A New Era in School Counseling

A Practical Guide

Second Edition

Rita Schellenberg

ROWMAN & LITTLEFIELD EDUCATION

A division of
ROWMAN & LITTLEFIELD PUBLISHERS, INC.
Lanham • New York • Toronto • Plymouth, UK

Published by Rowman & Littlefield Education
A division of Rowman & Littlefield Publishers, Inc.
A wholly owned subsidiary of The Rowman & Littlefield Publishing Group, Inc.
4501 Forbes Boulevard, Suite 200, Lanham, Maryland 20706
www.rowman.com

10 Thornbury Road, Plymouth PL6 7PP, United Kingdom

British Library Cataloguing in Publication Information Available

Library of Congress Cataloging-in-Publication Data
Schellenberg, Rita Cantrell.
  A new era in school counseling : a practical guide / Rita Schellenberg.—
Second edition.
     pages ; cm
  Includes bibliographical references and index.
  ISBN 978-1-4758-0450-8 (cloth : alk. paper)—ISBN 978-1-4758-0457-7
(pbk. : alk. paper)—ISBN 978-1-4758-0458-4 (ebook) 1. Educational
counseling—United States. 2. Student counselors—United States. I. Title.
  LB1027.5.S253 2013
  371.4—dc23   2013002020

∞TM The paper used in this publication meets the minimum requirements of
American National Standard for Information Sciences—Permanence of
Paper for Printed Library Materials, ANSI/NISO Z39.48-1992.

Printed in the United States of America

This text is dedicated to countless others who have sought to quench seemingly insatiable desires to improve school counselor education and practice.

Contents

CD Contents   vii

Preface: Evolutionary or Revolutionary?   ix

Frequently Used Acronyms   xiii

1   The New Era: A Preview   1

2   A Game Changer: The Needs of the Many   15

3   A Special Breed: Roles and Functions   27

4   Our Bread and Butter: Research and Program Evaluation   55

5   On Becoming the Quintessential New Era School Counselor   63

6   The Tool Box of the Century   81

Glossary   99

References   113

Index   119

About the Author   127

CD Contents

Action Plan Template: School Counseling Operational Plan for Effectiveness (SCOPE)

Case Notes (Essential Note-Keeping Elements)

Child Abuse Report (Suspected Child Abuse Reporting)

Core School Counseling Curriculum Communication to Teachers (Beginning of Year)

Informed Consent (Parental Consent for Small Groups/Individual Counseling Services)

Informed Consent (Parental Consent for Sensitive Classroom Lessons/Assemblies)

Opt Out of School Counseling Form

Referral for School Counseling Services by Teacher/Administrator

Referral for School Counseling Services by Parent

Referral for School Counseling Services (Elementary Student Self-Referral)

Referral for School Counseling Services (Secondary Student Self-Referral)

Release of School Counseling Case Notes and Sharing of Information

Results Report Template: School Counseling Operational Report of Effectiveness (SCORE)

Suicide Ideation Report (Suspected Suicide Reporting)

Preface: Evolutionary or Revolutionary?

Well school counselors, we are now more than a century young. Yes, I said, "young"—profession time! Only three editions into the American School Counselor Association (ASCA) National Model and we have made great strides toward unification and maturity. Remember, this is not a sprint, but a marathon. It took the Egyptian civilization a few centuries after unification to reach maturity—now that's quite a run!

The latest edition of the ASCA National Model reminds us of our extraordinary metamorphosis from "a position, to a service, to a program" (ASCA, 2012, p. vii). Still, *the times they are a-changin*—to borrow a few of the fitting and golden words of Bob Dylan. Thanks to the continued and unbridled efforts of countless leaders our next century promises to be just as evolutionary—perhaps revolutionary!

What can we expect in this new era of tireless dedication to improvement? The concept of closing the achievement gap will continue to be significant. That is, identifying your school's low-achieving student populations and providing responsive services to improve academic and post-secondary success will continue to be a priority. The new era will continue to underscore the importance of response to intervention, implementation of empirically validated approaches, program evaluation, and identification of research strategies for accountability and leadership. New era school counselors are called to magnify the focus on comprehensive program structure, purpose, and management that is preventative and developmental in nature, data-driven, results-oriented, and promotes student achievement. For these reasons, school counselors are being asked to heighten the emphasis on leadership, collaboration, advocacy, and systemic change as illustrated in ASCA National Model's trademark diamond graphic (ASCA, 2012).

In this new era, more so than in the past, the concept of universal academic achievement will be redefined. Our attention is called to strategies that not only identify and intervene in the lives of low-performing students, students with disabilities, and advanced-functioning students, but students who are not applying themselves to their fullest potential or those who are just getting by—sometimes referred to as the "invisible" student (Sink, 2011, p. ii). Uncovering and nurturing the strengths that might otherwise lie dormant in every student is vital to fueling our nation and growing our next world leaders.

This new era will also usher in a trend toward unfettering the vaulted topic historically viewed as taboo in the schools—spirituality. School counselors will ready themselves to address the diverse spiritual needs of students as a crucial cultural agent and developmental aspect of the human experience. Primary school counseling approaches for students of all ages and developmental levels will include positive behavioral support, exploring systems and applying behavioral strategies to mediate academic and behavioral concerns. Strength-based counseling, too, will become a commonly applied practice, exploring developmental assets to build resilience and fortify protective factors.

The anticipated explosion of technology over the next century necessitates a continued need to address the digital needs of students, including Internet safety and the appropriate uses of communication systems and social networking forums. Indeed, a new era school counselor for a new era of student—mind, body, and spirit.

This book continues to promote the transformation of our profession in what promises to be an unprecedented era by addressing the established and developing best practices significant to maturing the school counseling profession. In this way, *The New Era of School Counseling: A Practical Guide* is much like its predecessor, *The New School Counselor: Strategies for Universal Academic Achievement* (2008).

Also like its predecessor, this text uses a how-to-do-it approach with real-world applications that equip school counselors with the knowledge and strategies grounded in ASCA National Model (2012) and deemed essential by the Council for Accreditation of Counseling and Related Educational Programs (CACREP, 2009). The accompanying CD-ROM provides school counselors with more user-friendly action plans and results-report templates and additional forms to meet the rigorous demands and highest standards of practice. A glossary of frequently used terminology and a list of acronyms in school settings are new to this edition.

The ability of this text to bridge new era theory and practice also provides counselor educators and supervisors with experiential learning tools for optimal school counselor preparation. School administrators, too, will find this brief resource helpful in gaining a lucid understanding of the new era of school counseling and the contemporary roles and functions of the school counselor.

So, let us now embark upon this new era that promises heightened positive outcomes for professional practices. In doing so, we cannot continue business as usual. We are called to plow forward with unparalleled passion and selfless delight for chiseling a dynamic profession that frames school counselors as powerful and positive change agents. Might we also stir this passion in others—play Survivor's 1982 worldwide, certified platinum, top of the chart hit, "Eye of the Tiger," if you feel compelled!

Frequently Used Acronyms

Adapted from The School Counselor's Study Guide for Credentialing Exams, *Schellenberg, 2012*

AACD	American Association for Counseling and Development
AACE	Association for Assessment in Counseling and Education
ACA	American Counseling Association
ACES	Association for Counselor Education and Supervision
ACSCI	Association of Computer-Based Systems for Career Information
ACT	American College Testing
ADHD	Attention-Deficit/Hyperactivity Disorder
AMCD	Association for Multicultural Counseling and Development
AOD	Alcohol and Other Drugs
APGA	American Personnel and Guidance Association
ASCA	American School Counselor Association
ASGW	Association for Specialists in Group Work
ASVAB	Armed Services Vocational Aptitude Battery
BIP	Behavior Intervention Plan
CACGS	Computer-Assisted Career Guidance Systems
CACREP	Council for Accreditation of Counseling and Related Educational Programs
CAPTA	Child Abuse Prevention and Treatment Act
CIDS	Career Information Delivery Systems
CPCE	Counselor Preparation Comprehensive Examination
CPS	Child Protective Services

CSCORE	Center for School Counseling Outcome Research and Evaluation
ESEA	Elementary and Secondary Education Act
ELL	English Language Learners
ESL	English as a Second Language
FERPA	Family Educational Rights and Privacy Act
GATB	General Aptitude Test Battery
GED	General Equivalency Diploma
HIPAA	Health Insurance Portability and Accountability Act
IDEA	Individuals with Disabilities Education Act
IEP	Individualized Education Program/Plan
KOIS	Kuder Occupational Interest Survey
LEP	Limited English Proficient
MBTI	Myers-Briggs Type Indicator
MOS	Microsoft Office Specialist
NBCC	National Board for Certified Counselors
NBPTS	National Board for Professional Teaching Standards
NCATE	National Council for Accreditation of Teacher Education
NCC	National Certified Counselor
NCDA	National Career Development Association
NCE	National Counseling Examination
NCLB	No Child Left Behind
NCSC	National Certified School Counselor
NCSCE	National Certified School Counselor Examination
NCTSC	National Center for Transforming School Counseling
NOCTI	National Occupational Competency Testing Institute
NRF	National Retail Federation
NSCTI	National School Counselor Training Initiative
NTE	National Teachers Examination
O*Net	Occupational Information Network
PIAT	Peabody Individual Achievement Test
PSAT	Preliminary Scholastic Aptitude Test
PSC	Professional School Counselor
PTA	Parent Teacher Association
PTSA	Parent Teacher Student Association
REBT	Rational Emotive Behavior Therapy
SAT	Scholastic Aptitude Test
SCA	Student Council Association
SCALE	School Counseling Analysis, Leadership, and Evaluation

SCOPE	School Counseling Operational Plan for Effectiveness
SCORE	School Counseling Operational Report of Effectiveness
SDS	Self-Directed Search
SES	Socioeconomic Status
SII	Strong Interest Inventory
SOL	Standards of Learning
TSCI	Transforming School Counseling Initiative
WAIS	Wechsler Adult Intelligence Scale
WISC	Wechsler Intelligence Scale for Children

CHAPTER 1

The New Era: A Preview

Historically, school counseling has been primarily shaped by ever-changing social justice movements and educational reform initiatives. Over time, we have become more cautious in accommodating the educational reform du jour. Now on our third edition of the American School Counselor Association (ASCA) National Model (2012), this unifying professional framework guides our ability to accommodate an array of reform agendas that come our way by maintaining focus on growing a comprehensive school counseling program that takes a holistic and balanced approach to student development.

Traditionally, school counselors have viewed our function as indirectly increasing the academic achievement of students by removing physical, personal, social, emotional, and behavioral obstacles to learning using primarily "individual-focused interventions on behalf of selected students" (Paisley & Hayes, 2002, p. 1). Conversely, school administrators believe that the school counselor should function more systemically and "work with students to build skills that have a direct impact on school related work and functioning" (Shoffner & Williamson, 2000, p. 128). These fundamental philosophical differences coupled with our failure to appropriately articulate roles and functions resulted in a lack of understanding of what school counselors do, and more importantly *how* what we do is making a positive difference in the lives of students, families, and the communities we serve.

The powerful impetus behind crucial, fundamental changes in the school counseling profession was prompted by a report published in 1987 by the American Counseling Association (ACA) titled *School*

Counseling: A Profession at Risk. The undeniable and disturbing realities outlined by the ACA (www.counseling.org) regarding a profession viewed as withering, unnecessary, and diagnosed to decay prompted immediate and unremitting action on the part of concerned stakeholders. Thanks to well-planned treatment, we achieved a favorable prognosis, but we are not out of the woods yet.

The profession has closed the philosophical divides and more closely aligned school counseling with the mission of schools. However, there is still work to be done and some in our ranks who are resistant to change.

We can no longer be viewed as nice, but not necessary. This will require a united front. That is, traditionalists are called to jump on board with new-vision school counselors and embark upon the new era, establishing comprehensive school counseling programs that promote academic achievement while balancing the holistic needs of students.

We can begin by emphasizing the changed language of our profession. Terminology helps to define a profession and strengthen professional identity. Terms such as *guidance services* and *guidance counselor* are Jurassic and no longer reflect the comprehensive nature of school counseling programs and our dual roles of educator and counselor. Nonetheless, many within and outside of the school community continue to use these outdated terms generally due to force of habit. Using the adage familiar to many—it is time to kick the habit! The support of school administrators can make all the difference.

If we are to promote the use of contemporary school counseling language and school counselor roles and functions (discussed in chapter 3), then leadership alliances with administrators need to be established and maintained. School counselors begin by providing administrators with a thorough understanding of contemporary school counseling. In doing so, it is crucial to reveal evidence of outcomes that demonstrate how the school counseling program is contributing to academic and postsecondary achievement as well as holistic student development and well-being—our contemporary comprehensive roles and functions. Only then can we influence the mighty and deeply seeded beliefs of administrators, who may continue to view school counseling programs as ancillary. Only then can we alter the trajectory of school counseling and sustain a comprehensive school counseling program that provides students (and all stakeholders) with the highest quality educational services. Ralph Waldo Emerson may have said it best: "This time, like all other times, is a very good one, if we but know what to do with it."

FORCES SHAPING A MATURING PROFESSION

Now is not the time for complacency but a time to break free from ruts—to act upon the present so as to influence the future. The past offers insights from which to learn, the inspiration from which to grow, the strength to trudge forward, and the knowledge to pass along to future generations. Change can be frightening, but fleeting moments of fervent courage can result in great things.

Transforming School Counseling Initiative and the ASCA

Soon after the publication of *School Counseling: A Profession at Risk* (ACA, 1987), ASCA began creating monographs, position papers, role statements, revised program philosophies, and a series of recommendations to include school counselors as key players in educational reform initiatives. ASCA adopted national standards and developed a national model to aid in unifying the profession and to serve as a guide to comprehensive developmental practices. The Education Trust (1997), too, introduced the Transforming School Counseling Initiative (TSCI).

The TSCI introduced a new paradigm to replace the existing paradigm and immediately began emphasizing the importance of school counseling leadership, support for academic- and systems-focused programming, and the need to make adequate yearly progress. Together, the visionary super powers of ASCA and the TSCI served as rutbusters, redefining the roles and functions of the school counselor within the context of a new vision that more closely aligns school counseling with the academic mission of schools.

The new paradigm shifts the focus of school counseling away from mental health and toward academic achievement, away from the individual student and toward the whole school. Those attached to the traditional mental health–focused paradigm argue that the new paradigm is too academic-focused, ignoring the mental health needs of students. Proponents of new vision school counseling argue that the new paradigm does not represent a flatlining of mental health services, but resuscitates those services to more fully and adequately meet the mental health needs of students through collaboration and referral.

Contrary to some interpretations, this new vision school counselor does not represent an abandonment of concern for the personal and social development of children and adolescents. Instead, it reflects the requirement that school counselors link interventions to the mission and purposes of schooling while holding themselves accountable for their contributions to student outcomes (Paisley & Hayes, 2003, p. 200).

New vision school counseling requires a belief in the capacity of all students at varying developmental stages to obtain high levels of academic achievement and meaningful futures in a global economy and technologically advanced world, overcoming obstacles to life success. This growing breed of school counselor engages in systemic leadership, advocacy, collaboration, consultation, counseling, coordination, assessment, and data analysis. Serving as social action and change agents, new vision school counselors identify and remove inequities and other barriers to academic achievement while simultaneously meeting the mental health needs of students.

The application of new vision school counseling requires knowledge and skills in developing and evaluating programs that are needs- and data-driven, standards-based, research-supported, and academic- and systemic-focused. School counselors document these accountable practices and programming outcomes, including closing the achievement gap strategies, using action plans, lesson plans, and results reports (ASCA, 2012).

Prior to the TSCI, school counselor training programs generally applied a clinical, mental health pedagogy and an individualistic focus with little or no emphasis on standards, systems, technology, the use of data, academic achievement, program evaluation, evidence-based practices, and data reporting. Therefore, many currently practicing school counselors lack the preparation and understanding of the roles and functions of the contemporary, academic-focused school counselor and the tools and approaches for demonstrating accountable practices as we enter the next era of school counseling. What's more, since practice informs academic theory, paradoxically, deficits in practice create deficits in school counselor education resulting in the absence of applied new vision approaches and models for the optimal preparation of future school counselors.

While the TSCI was actually established with the express purpose of restructuring school counselor education at the graduate level, the TSCI recognizes the need to close this preparation gap between school counselors trained under the traditional model and those trained under the new vision model. For that reason, the TSCI partnered with Metropolitan Life Insurance Company (MetLife) to fund the development of the National School Counselor Training Initiative (NSCTI) and the National Center for Transforming School Counseling (NCTSC) located at www.edtrust.org/dc/tsc.

The NSCTI and NCTSC developed and disseminated four modules that instruct practicing school counselors in the components of the TSCI new vision. The modules challenge school counselor belief systems and describe how school counselors can contribute to the high academic achievement of and obtain educational equity for all students through both systemic and individual leadership, advocacy, and collaboration.

The MetLife initiative also addresses systemic inequities, social justice, diversity, accountable practices, and technological competence.

Center for School Counseling Outcome Research and Evaluation (CSCORE)

The Center for School Counseling Outcome Research and Evaluation (CSCORE, 2000), formerly known as the Center for School Counseling Outcome Research (CSCOR), was established during a TSCI summer conference for the purpose of providing school counselor leadership in establishing accountable practices. The center is part of the School of Education at the University of Massachusetts (www. umass.edu/schoolcounseling).

CSCORE focuses on providing resources to assist school counselors in grounding practices in research and standards, conducting program evaluation, and administering valid outcome measures. The center publishes quarterly research briefs for school counseling practitioners to increase knowledge regarding ways in which school counselors can implement academic- and systems-focused practices and support strategies for closing the achievement gap. CSCORE advocates for new era school counseling practices by (1) assisting efforts to ensure that all students achieve academically, (2) emphasizing the importance of systemic interventions, and (3) focusing on the importance of using research to guide practice, monitor effectiveness, and evaluate student learning outcomes.

Association for Counselor Education and Supervision (ACES) and the Council for Accreditation of Counseling and Related Educational Programs (CACREP)

The Association for Counselor Education and Supervision (ACES) is a division of the ACA. The purpose of ACES (www.acesonline.net) is to provide leadership and continuous improvement in the education, credentialing, and supervision of counselors in diverse specialty settings. Committed to the advancement of counselor education and supervision, ACES began the accreditation of counseling programs, which laid the foundation for its successor the Council for Accreditation of Counseling and Related Educational Programs (CACREP).

In 1978, CACREP (www.cacrep.org) was formed to standardize training and function as the primary accrediting body for counselor education programs. In 2001, CACREP published standards that reflected the new vision's academic- and systems-focused paradigm. In 2009, CACREP revised those standards to continue reflecting the contemporary practices of counseling and counseling specialties taking into account current developments and future trends. The 2009 standards emphasize the professional identity of counselor and the importance of measuring student learning outcomes.

CACREP provides counselor education programs with unified, minimal competencies for the optimal preparation of school counselors. CACREP requires demonstrated knowledge in eight core areas of counselor education (i.e., professional orientation and ethical practice, social and cultural diversity, human growth and development, career development, helping relationships, group work, assessment, and research and program evaluation). Those studying to become school counselors must also master each of the eight school counseling specialty standards:

1. the foundations of school counseling
2. counseling prevention and intervention
3. diversity and advocacy
4. assessment
5. research and evaluation
6. academic development
7. collaboration and consultation
8. leadership

These school counseling specialty standards emphasize education and training in developing a comprehensive, developmentally appropriate school counseling program using evidence-based prevention and intervention practices that meet the needs of diverse students. The standards further underscore the importance of using a program model (e.g., ASCA National Model) in both school counselor education and school counseling practices. CACREP also spotlights the importance of academic outcomes and demonstrating the use of data-driven and data-producing programs, and program evaluation in school counseling practices. The standards further emphasize the importance of identifying and removing personal and systemic barriers to academic achievement.

CACREP has grown steadily for the past thirty years, accrediting the majority of institutions that offer counselor education programs (Ritchie & Bobby, 2011). "CACREP has become a university magnet with schools across the country seeking its stamp of approval. Indeed, if school counselor education were a religion, CACREP would be our bible, with counselor educators striving to live by the word" (Schellenberg, 2012, p. 6).

National Board for Certified Counselors (NBCC)

Gladding (2001) defines certification as the process by which an agency, government, or association officially grants recognition to an individual for having met certain professional qualifications that have been developed by the profession. NBCC (www.nbcc.org) is the national professional certification board that monitors the certification system for counselors and maintains a national register of certified counselors. In addition to national credentialing, NBCC examinations are used by more than forty-eight states to credential professional counselors on a state level. NBCC was created by the ACA and both organizations work closely to advance the profession of counseling and maintain high standards of excellence.

Counselors who hold the voluntary National Certified Counselor (NCC) credential from the National Board for Certified Counselors (NBCC) have demonstrated mastery of the CACREP standards as well as the NBCC standards. Consequently, school counselors, who hold the NCC credential have established equivalency to graduation from a CACREP accredited program as well as mastery of the high standards set by the profession.

The NBCC administers specialty counseling credentials such as the National Certified School Counselor (NCSC) credential first awarded in 1991. The NCC is a prerequisite or corequisite for the NCSC. School counselors who hold the NCSC have demonstrated competence in areas specific to contemporary school counseling and demonstrate a high level of professional commitment that goes beyond required state licensing.

The NBCC requires a master's degree and uses the CACREP standards, ASCA program standards, formal practices statements, and national studies to create NCSC requirements and assessment. The NCSC is a product of a collaborative effort between key professional counseling organizations and supported by CACREP and ACES.

The NBCC and the National Board for Professional Teaching Standards (NBPTS) began working together to create an advanced credential for school counselors that would tie school counseling standards to the NBPTS requirements. Negotiations ended unsuccessfully in 2003 when NBCC would not agree to (1) an advanced counselor credential controlled by a sixty-three-member board of teachers with only one school counselor representative, (2) an advanced counselor credential that does not require a master's degree, and (3) an advanced school counseling credential that is not a collaborative effort with all professional associations, accreditation, and certification organizations in counseling.

The NBPTS is a teacher certification board/association that promotes the school counselor as educator. CACREP, NBCC, and ASCA are counselor accrediting, certification, and professional associations that promote the school counselor's professional identity of counselor. Understanding that first and foremost school counselors are counselors, CACREP, NBCC, and ASCA recognize both our roles of educator and counselor in defining our specialty. School counselors focus on academic achievement, but in relation to the provision of sound counseling services that are within the scope of school counseling discussed later in this text. Educators understand the priorities—student safety first—always. Counselor educators, parents, teachers, and school administrators desire instructional competence in a school counselor, but need clinical counseling competence in a school counselor, who is often the only mental health professional in the school building. And unfortunately, even with the application of a collaborative model, the only counselor a troubled child or adolescent may ever see is the school counselor.

An advanced school counselor credential that is not governed by counselors and the counseling profession, and is grounded in the core propositions of *what teachers should know and be able to do* may not inspire the public's confidence in the school counselor's clinical ability to meet the personal, social, and emotional needs of children. This is particularly significant in a charged climate where the public's confidence in our educational system is already wavering if not waning. Parents are not only questioning the ability of public schools to successfully educate their child, but the ability of public schools to identify and effectively intervene in situations with troubled students who threaten the safety of their child.

Whether one holds the philosophy that a school counselor is a counselor placed in a school setting, or an educator who applies counseling skills, the counseling component and counselor identity must be equally advanced and empowered. As such, one credential must not be pitted against the other or supported more than the other. Both credentials are valuable in establishing the school counselor's advanced knowledge and expertise in counseling and teaching/learning. Currently, however, the majority of states provide incentives for only the NBPTS-certified school counselor, perpetuating school counselors' blurred perceptions of professional identity. Exclusive support for primarily teacher-controlled NBPTS school counseling credential may also be perceived as an implied belief that instructional competence supersedes clinical and counseling competence, trumping student safety.

The U.S. House of Representatives Committee on Appropriations voiced concern regarding the NBPTS's credentialing of school counselors, encouraging the NBPTS to retain its intended focus—to improve the skills and credentials of classroom teachers (U.S. House of Representatives, 2006). Acting on this concern the House Committee on Appropriations has provided more flexibility to the Department of Education with regard to the earmarking of advanced credential funding. This House Committee action may open the door to school administrators and all stakeholders to advocate for the recognition of the NBCC's school counselor credential as well as the NBPTS school counselor credential when providing incentives and financial supplements for the advanced credentialing of school counselors.

American School Counselor Association (ASCA)

ASCA provides professional development, leadership, advocacy, research, publications, and resources to school counselors worldwide. Many of their resources do not require association membership in order to gain access at www.schoolcounselor.org.

ASCA adopted national standards (Campbell & Dahir, 1997) and created a national model (ASCA, 2012) to include those standards. The ASCA national model aids in unifying our professional identity and practices and serves as a framework from which to establish accountable, comprehensive, developmental school counseling programs.

The national model provides standards, competencies, and indicators for facilitating student development in three domains (i.e., academic, career, personal/social). The model also includes school counselor performance standards that reflect contemporary roles and functions for the new era in school counseling.

ASCA provides school counseling practitioners and counselor educators with interactive tools such as the School Counseling Analysis, Leadership and Evaluation (SCALE) Research Center. School counselors can link to the center from the main ASCA Web page previously noted. SCALE is dedicated to providing resources to support results-based, comprehensive school counseling programs. The system identifies potential research partners, grants, and professional development opportunities. ASCA Scene, too, allows school counselors and counselor educators to interact with others and the system to get information and resources to support professional roles and functions. ASCA Scene provides a massive file cabinet of materials for practice, discussion groups, webinar listings, and membership profiles for professional networking.

ACHIEVING ACADEMIC-FOCUSED SCHOOL COUNSELING

ASCA and TSCI call for an alignment with academic achievement missions and programming that includes strategies to help close the achievement gap. The ASCA National Model (2012) is supported by CACREP, professional school counseling associations, and a substantial body of research and literature. Embracing an academic-focused model for school counseling is further supported by research that links student academic success to collaborative school cultures that exude an academic emphasis (Goddard, Hoy, & Woolfolk, 2000).

Failure of the mental health model to align school counseling with the mission of schools and to demonstrate an impact on academic achievement is chronicled in professional literature and exemplified in the historical exclusion of school counselors in educational reform agendas. The direction of the profession has been slow to turn, but it is turning.

It takes time to apply theory to practice. Attaching school counseling to school reform initiatives and to the educational system as a whole requires changes in counselor education, practice, and leadership, as well as practical tools and approaches. School counselors have been astutely careful not to neglect the personal, social, and emotional needs of children and adolescents while also attending to academic achievement.

Alas, time has not been the only barrier to more academic-focused practices. Some counselor educators and school counseling practitioners have been resistant to the paradigm switch, preferring to adhere to the traditional model for what is likely a multitude of reasons that include a lack of motivation toward change in general.

For these die-hard traditionalists not hardwired to change the shift has been akin to the explosive divide of a ballistic missile albeit friendly fire. Providentially, a lack of support from school counseling professionals intent upon traditional practices has been met by an unequivocal force—school administrators.

School Administrator and School Counselor Leadership Alliance

Professional school counseling alliances have been forged and are acting as resolute and progressive forces, switching the paradigm and reversing the direction of passé school counseling practices. The involvement and support of school administrators is essential to building a comprehensive school counseling program that is effective, evolving, and systems-focused.

School boards, superintendents, and school principals determine the roles and functions of school counselors within a division. Therefore, implementation of a comprehensive school counseling program that balances the career, academic, and personal-social development of students depends upon the acceptance, support, and collective leadership of school administrators and school counseling practitioners.

Historically, school administrators come from teacher backgrounds and receive minimal training in educational leadership programs on the perspectives of school personnel other than teachers. As such, school administrators have had limited opportunities to fully understand the roles and functions of the school counselor as delineated by the school counseling profession.

School counselors, many of whom were schooled under the traditional pedagogy and prior to the establishment of the national school counseling standards and ASCA national model, are also unable to clearly articulate professional roles, functions, identity, goals, and direction in this new era. As a result, school administrators have been relegated to the position of spectator, despite supervisory responsibilities and a vested interest in integrating this disconnected and specialized subset into the educational system.

Therefore, the first barrier to overcome in establishing a school counselor and school administrator alliance is a mutual understanding of the independent and interdependent functions of each of the system's components. Appreciating this interconnectedness and understanding that changes in one component (school counseling programs) have consequences for the whole (school missions) is vital to positive systemic change. Fittingly, the systems-integration philosophies of W. Edwards Deming have been likened to the contemporary leadership role of school administrators.

> Systems thinking is like conducting a piece of music for an orchestra. . . . [E]ach element can function apart from the others. . . . [T]he flute solo may be pleasant, the percussion powerful, the strings, in perfect harmony . . . it is the work of the conductor who pulls all the parts together into one beautiful song. Only then do the musicians—and the audience members—get the full and intended effect. When the parts are working together as a thriving whole under the direction of a skilled school leader, the district becomes more effective. (Sutton, 2006, p. 47)

School administrators are being challenged to ensure a standards-based curriculum, heighten accountability, and integrate specialized resources and manpower to bring about monumental systemic change in education. School counselors are being called upon to engage those specialized skills in counseling and education and to connect to the system in order to align with school missions and to directly impact global student achievement using accountable practices. For the first time in history, school administrator and school counselor paradigms, perspectives, and goals are homogenous, making leadership alliances not only possible but probable and uniquely powerful in this next era.

SUMMARY

In order to survive as a profession and to meet the diverse needs of students in today's educational climate, school counselor education and practice must switch paradigms from the traditional mental health–focused model that serves a selected few to the new academic-focused paradigm that serves the many and better aligns with the academic achievement mission of schools. Despite support for the new paradigm from the major forces that shape the profession of school counseling, some counselor educators and practitioners are content to continue promoting the outdated, unsuccessful mental health model. Emphasis is placed on school administrator–school counselor alliances to ensure the implementation of comprehensive school counseling programs that attend to total student development while also enhancing academic achievement through both direct and indirect student services.

School counselors promote needs-driven, standards-based, account-able programming that aligns comprehensive school counseling pro-grams with academic achievement missions and contribute to closing the achievement gap. An immediate need exists for school counselor–school administrator partnerships and holistic approaches that meet the career, personal-social, and academic development of students as well as practical tools for daily practice and data reporting.

CHAPTER 2

A Game Changer: The Needs of the Many

Once a profession focused on providing guidance services and responding to the individual mental health needs of a select few, the paradigm switch to a more balanced approach that meets the needs of the many was a game-changer for the school counseling profession. The passage from individual to system, from guidance to comprehensive school counseling services, and from a mental health focus to a more balanced approach that aligns with the academic achievement mission of schools has been an extraordinary journey.

Collaboration and consultation with stakeholders—namely school administrators, parents, teachers, and members of the community—has become essential to developing and strengthening a school counseling program that meets the customized and holistic needs of diverse students and unique school environments. The school counseling program does not belong to the school counselor; it belongs to the stakeholders. In fact, ASCA recommends establishing an advisory council in which stakeholder membership is representative of the community's diversity.

The ASCA National Model (2012) provides guidelines for creating a viable school counseling advisory council that promotes system perspectives by involving diverse stakeholders. Identifying stakeholder needs also requires the ability to create and conduct needs assessments and the ability to identify and analyze existing relevant data sources within and outside of the school and division. Information obtained from data collection and analysis aids school counselors in designing or redesigning programs for targeted topics and populations and allow for continuous program improvement.

DATA-DRIVEN PROGRAM PLANNING

The powerful smack of hard data provides us with the sobering clarity needed to make informed decisions that positively impact comprehensive school counseling programs. The study of data can reveal stakeholder needs, inequities in programming and practices, and other barriers to academic achievement and student development essential to targeted, goal-focused practices.

ASCA recommends that school counselors use three types of data to identify stakeholder needs, areas of concern, and to evaluate services and program effectiveness. Process data identifies the manner in which the program was implemented and how many participants were impacted. Process data endeavors to answer the question, "What did you do for whom?" and provides evidence that an event occurred (ASCA, 2012, p. 51). Perception data endeavors to answer the question, "What do people think they know, believe or can do?" (ASCA, 2012, p. 51). Perception data generally includes data obtained from self-reports, surveys, pre-post measures, needs assessments. While perception and process data are useful for program improvement and duplication, outcome data is essential to establishing *how* the school counseling activity made a difference and to what extent—effectiveness. Outcome data demonstrates program impact and endeavors to answer the question, "So what?" (ASCA, 2012, p. 52). Examples of outcome data include attendance and graduation rates, promotion and retention rates, standardized test scores, and grade point averages.

School counselors, who make use of the robust cornucopia of existing data sources have a fountain flowing with opportunity for needs identification, accountable program planning, implementation, and evaluation. When using existing data sources, school counselors look for patterns and inconsistencies. The following list includes potential achievement and behavioral data sources generally available to school counselors.

- Academic Portfolio Goals Completion
- Attendance Rates
- Career and Technical Education Program Participation
- Career Assessments
- Career Portfolio–Career Action Plan Goal Completion

- Classroom Performance Data
- College Acceptance Rates
- Conflict Resolution/Peer Mediation Records
- Consultation
- Course Enrollment Patterns
- Demographic Data
- Discipline Records
- Drop-out Rates
- Drug Violations
- Expulsion Records
- Financial Data
- Grade Reports
- Graduation Rates
- Homework Completion Records
- Industry Certification Participation/Pass Rates
- Interest Inventories
- Needs Assessment
- Nontraditional Program Track (GED, job corps, etc.)
- Parent/Community School Involvement–Volunteer Data
- Parent-Teacher Conference Records
- Pre- and Post-program Knowledge/Skills Measure
- Program Completions (GED, honors)
- Promotion and Retention Rates
- PTA/PTSA Attendance Rates
- Scholarship Records
- School Event Attendance Rates
- Scores on the GED Official Practice Test
- Self-Assessment
- Standardized Assessment Data/Test Scores
- Student Community Service/Volunteer Data
- Student Extracurricular Activities Participation
- Suspensions (in-school)
- Suspensions (out-of-school)
- Time-out Records

School counselors can leverage the power of information technology to mine the seemingly unlimited amounts of information for data-driven program planning that can be used to inform and improve educational practices. Data-based decision making in education has been defined as the "process of collecting, analyzing, reporting, and using data for school improvement" (Poynton & Carey, 2006, p. 121).

Many data-based decision-making models are available for school counselors to use as a framework for facilitating the process. Poynton and Carey (2006) provide school counselors with a review of data-based decision-making models both within and outside of school counseling. It is prudent to capture data from multiple sources in order to clarify needs and identify levels of need for timely, successful programming. For this reason a combination of both existing data and needs assessment approaches can provide powerful support for programming.

Needs Assessment Instruments/Techniques

Stakeholder needs may be assessed using existing data, as previously noted, or by gathering data in the form of participant perceptions from the target population using a needs assessment technique or instrument. Needs assessments techniques/instruments are time-honored means by which school counselors can identify and target relevant needs for appropriate programming. Needs assessments are generally used to systematically identify the needs of broader populations (e.g., student body, teachers, parents, community agencies) and subpopulations (e.g., special education students, fifth grade teachers, parents of gifted students, mental health agencies).

Assessing needs based on participant perceptions is not generally considered standardized, but can take a more formal tone versus an informal tone. Assessment instruments and techniques may be written (e.g., survey, questionnaire) or oral (e.g., interview), and conducted in person, on the telephone, via the Internet, or by mail. When assessing needs based on participant perception, the school counselor might elect to use focus groups, community forums, and/or key informants.

School counselors, who elect to use focus groups, select multiple individuals representative of the population to be served—much like apple picking. Collectively, in a structured or semistructured format, diverse needs are discussed and the group prioritizes needs. If you picked any bad apples, this is where you'll find out! Community forums have merit due to the inclusive nature of the approach. Any stakeholder wishing to be involved may participate. School counselors announce the topic to be discussed and meeting dates and times. Those interested participate in much the same fashion as the focus group. Key informants are selected by the school counselor. Selection is based on the potential participant's level of knowledge of the target population. The participant may or may not be a member of the population, but most have an in-depth knowledge of the target population. Key informants are typically surveyed individually or in small groups.

Initial needs assessments administered to adult stakeholders might begin with general questions. Responses to the initial questions might suggest a need for more specific follow-up questions vital to targeted, needs-driven programming and identifying best practices. The following sampling of questions would be considered appropriate for assessing the needs of upper elementary school students, adults, and students at the high school level:

- What school counseling services do you find helpful?
- What additional school counseling services would you find helpful?
- What are the strengths of the school counseling program?
- What suggestions do you have for possible improvements to the school counseling program?
- What questions do you have regarding the school counseling program and services?
- What are some ways you would like to become involved in the school counseling program?
- What barriers to student development have you observed or do you believe exist in our school?
- What suggestions do you have for the school counseling program for removing such barriers?

Needs assessments for children may be read aloud with interpretations depending upon developmental level. Needs assessments that make use of the check system are ideal for children and special-needs populations. For example, simply list the topics and have students place a check in the box beside the topic(s) of interest:

☐ Dealing with Bullies
☐ Safety (including Internet Safety)
☐ Nutrition and Health
☐ Study Skills and Organization
☐ Test-Taking Skills
☐ Making and Keeping Friends
☐ Self-Control
☐ Managing Time
☐ Managing Anger
☐ Communication
☐ Career
☐ Conflict Resolution/Peer Mediation (Getting Along)
☐ Problem Solving
☐ Decision Making (Making Good Choices)
☐ Self-Esteem (Liking Myself)
☐ Managing Stress (Expressing Feelings)
☐ Setting and Achieving Goals

The check system also allows for ease of administration. The school counselor may find it useful to combine elements of both structures based on intended purpose and population.

TRANSLATING NEEDS INTO GOALS AND MEASURABLE OBJECTIVES

Once the school counselor has an understanding of systemic programming based on stakeholder needs, those needs are translated into goal(s) that are supported by measurable objectives. For example, a goal based on need might be to reduce school-wide conflict. The goal does not lend itself to measurement; that is the task of the objective. Therefore, once a goal(s) is established, specific and measurable objectives that support goal achievement are developed.

One possible objective supporting this goal might be "students will be able to identify three conflict resolution strategies." We conclude, then, that there must be at least three conflict resolution strategies cov-

Table 2.1.   Who? How? and What? of Objectives

(W) *Who* are the participants receiving the program/intervention?

  Who examples:

  "Students will"
  "Teachers will"
  "Parents will"

(H) *How* will we know the behavior is achieved?

  How examples:

  "Students will identify"
  "Parents will be able to"
  "Teachers will develop"

(W) *What* is the desired behavior?

  What examples:

  "Students will identify five study skills strategies"
  "Parents will be able to define ADHD"
  "Teachers will develop five auditory teaching strategies"

ered in the curriculum content—brainiacs indeed! Research-supported curriculum development is discussed later in this chapter.

ASCA provides school counselors with broad goals (e.g., standards) and objectives (i.e., student competencies) that cover the three broad domains for a developmental comprehensive school counseling program. However, school counselors must also develop their own more specific and measurable objectives based on stakeholder need. Understanding how to translate stakeholder needs into goals and measurable learning objectives is crucial to creating program content that targets those needs. Table 2.1 describes a method for creating measurable objectives using a (W)ho, (H)ow, and (W)hat process.

RESEARCH-SUPPORTED CURRICULUM DEVELOPMENT

Once stakeholder needs are translated into goal(s) and measurable objectives, program content is created that supports the goal(s) and objectives. For example, if the goal is to improve student study skills, a measurable objective supporting this goal might be "students will identify five study skills strategies." The curriculum will include research-supported content and activities specific to achieving this objective. That is, the content will, in some manner, introduce five research-supported study skills strategies for improved study skills, ideally with this specific population.

Let's consider the concept of self-esteem. Negative self-esteem has had a long and prosperous career in invading hearts and minds with self-destructive rubbish, making "self" our best friend or our worst enemy. The benefits of positive self-esteem are as widely recognized as the entertaining Geico gecko for offering an insurance policy that kicks-in when life serves up spontaneous catastrophe (Schellenberg, 2012). With the help of research, school counselors reveal the link between self-esteem and personal-social, career, and academic development. The school counselor will seek to underscore the relationship between academic success and self-esteem to demonstrate a clear alignment with the academic mission of schools.

Once this link is established, research-supported interventions that have been successful in building a positive self-esteem are identified. Unlike the murmurs of idle gossip, research communicates factual information that demonstrates evidence-based techniques, models, and approaches, identifying what works and with whom—*best practices* (Schellenberg, 2012). To apply best practices, school counselors critically evaluate important components of relevant studies such as (1) theoretical orientation, (2) target population, (3) intervention used, (4) method of data collection and analysis, and (5) results. Again, using the construct/topic of self-esteem as our example, the following questions might aid in guiding school counselors toward this end:

- Does a correlation exist between self-esteem and academic performance?
- What does the research say about the academic proficiency of students who have a negative self-esteem versus those who have a positive self-esteem?
- Is poor self-esteem considered a barrier to academic achievement? If so, would it be logical to conclude that programs that enhance self-esteem remove a barrier to academic achievement?
- Which counseling and instructional interventions have been used in the past with positive outcomes?

- With what populations were the counseling and instructional interventions successful?

When developing curriculum, school counselors are sensitive to the diverse learning needs of students. School counselors accommodate the variety of learning styles and learning levels of students. School counselors are also careful to consider the theory of multiple intelligences when seeking to create lessons and group sessions geared toward holistic student development.

Howard Gardner (1983) contends that human cognition consists of eight independent, yet interactive intelligences across a variety of disciplines. Gardner defines intelligence as "biopsychological potential to process information that can be activated in a cultural setting to solve problems or create products that are of value in a culture" (Gardner & Moran, 2006, p. 227). These eight intelligences (i.e., linguistic, logical-mathematical, musical, spatial, bodily kinesthetic, naturalistic, interpersonal, and intrapersonal) are described in Table 2.2.

Table 2.2. Gardner's Eight Multiple Intelligences

Intelligence	Description
Linguistic	Reliance of spoken and written words; individuals generally adept in reading, writing, and speaking.
Logical-mathematical	Reliance on reasoning, numbers, and logic; individuals generally adept in scientific thinking, investigation, and making complex calculations.
Musical	Reliance on rhythmic sounds, pitch, and tones; individuals generally adept in singing, playing musical instruments, and composing music.
Spatial	Reliance on the mind's eye; individuals generally adept in design, puzzles, and navigation.
Bodily Kinesthetic	Reliance on touch and movement; individuals generally adept in dance and sports.
Naturalistic	Reliance on nurturing and that which is associated with nature; individuals generally adept at classifying organisms and understanding of the natural environment.
Interpersonal	Reliance on interactions with others; individuals generally adept at identifying the needs of others and working cooperatively with others.
Intrapersonal	Reliance on introspection, intuition, and self-reflection; individuals generally adept in understanding self and self control.

Source: Adapted from Gardner, H., & Moran, S. (2006). The science of multiple intelligences theory: A response to Lynn Waterhouse. *Educational Psychologist, 41*(4), 227–232.

The interactive nature of multiple intelligences offers insight into the workings of the human mind. Whether intriguing or deeply disturbing this information is nothing less than invaluable in developing and delivering curriculum that nurtures the diverse intelligences for optimal cognitive and affective learning experiences and sound career decision making.

Benjamin S. Bloom (1953) describes six classifications of learning levels progressing from the most basic to the most complex in hierarchical order: knowledge, comprehension, application, analysis, synthesis, evaluation. Bloom's Taxonomy has been revised to associate specific verbs that represent ways to promote the development of higher-level thinking skills at each level (Anderson & Krathwohl, 2001) as illustrated in Figure 2.1.

Robert Marzano's (2004) frequently applied instructional strategies have been empirically validated as approaches that build background knowledge and improve student achievement across grade levels. These strategies are listed in Table 2.3.

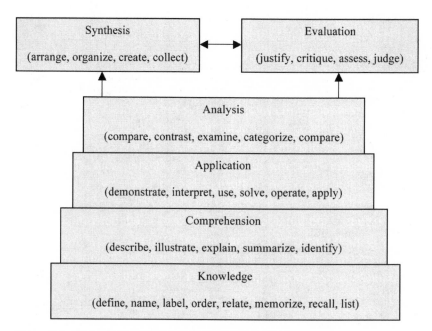

Figure 2.1. Bloom's Taxonomy and Associated Verbs

Table 2.3. Marzano's Nine Instructional Strategies

Instructional Strategy	Characteristics
Identifying similarities and differences	Breaking concepts into similar and dissimilar pieces; representing concepts in graphic forms (e.g., Venn diagrams, charts, analogies).
Summarizing and note taking	Conceptualizing presented material then restating it in one's own words; when note taking, more notes are better and allow time to process.
Reinforcing effort and providing recognition	Show the connection between effort and achievement (e.g., share success stories, underscore student's achievements); recognize individual accomplishments and personalize recognitions.
Homework and practice	Amount of homework should vary by grade level; homework schedule and setting should be consistent; homework provides practice; provide feedback on homework in a variety of ways.
Nonlinguistic representations	Use with linguistic representations; nonlinguistic representations stimulate and increase brain activity; use tangible models, physical movement, and apply symbols to represent words/images.
Cooperative learning	Positive impact on learning; vary group sizes and objectives.
Setting objectives and providing feedback	Provides direction for learning; students should personalize goals; use contracts; feedback should be timely, specific, and rubric based.
Generating and testing hypotheses	Use general rules to make a prediction; student should explain their predictions.
Cues, questions, and advanced organizers	Students use background knowledge to enhance learning; expose students to material prior to their learning it (e.g., create a graphic image, tell a story).

Source: Adapted from Marzano, R. J. (2004). *Building background knowledge for academic achievement: Research on what works in schools.* Alexandria, VA: Association for Supervision and Curriculum Development.

Lastly, the theory of learning style contends that individuals have a propensity toward receiving and storing information using one or more of three sensory modalities: visual (e.g., pictures, written word), kinesthetic (e.g., body movement, tactile), and auditory (e.g., spoken word). It is important for school counselors to gain a working knowledge of these learning styles and to teach students to identify their learning styles so that students might learn how to learn.

Individuals also have a preference for particular learning environments and times of day. Helping students to identify those conditions will promote optimal learning and adaptation to diverse teaching environments and tasks.

SUMMARY

The school counseling program belongs to the stakeholders. The school counselor actively seeks to identify stakeholder needs using data analysis and data collection. A multitude of potential data sources are available for assessing stakeholder need as well as the time-honored methods for needs assessments. Data allows school counselors to target specific needs and populations and to prioritize programming. Data allows school counselors to meet the needs of the system, while also assessing the system for barriers to student achievement and well-being.

Once school counselors have identified needs, goals, and measurable objectives, the research-supported curriculum becomes the focus. Best practices necessitate that school counselors become savvy consumers of research in order to explore, identify, and apply research-supported prevention and intervention strategies and to create research-based curriculum. School counselors also apply a working knowledge of learning styles, learning levels, and multiple intelligences when creating curriculum that is sensitive to the diverse needs of students.

counselor. Conceptualization of the dual roles of the school counselor can be summarized as follows: school counselors are both counselors and educators in a school setting who focus on the student as a learner, with school counseling services designed, delivered, and documented in an accountable manner that directly and indirectly advances academic achievement, enhances student development and well-being, and informs important others.

School counselors integrate the dual roles of educator and counselor into a succinct guiding philosophy that drives the affective and cognitive domains of programming and professional practices. The philosophy might be encapsulated as follows: a healthy mind is an educable mind and a healthy mind is not defined as free from physical, mental, emotional, social, and environmental distress. The progress made in this new era of school counseling rests in the school counselor's ability to embrace this belief and to integrate skills as educators and counselors to meet the academic, career, and personal/social development needs of today's diverse youth.

The adept school counselor moves fluently between the two roles for optimal student development. Sustaining this noble philosophy are accountable practices that demonstrate the direct impact of comprehensive school counseling programs on student academic achievement and total student development on a systems level.

As counselors and educators, school counselors engage in shared functions. These functions include the following: teaming, consulting, informing, collaborating, leading, advocating, counseling, programming, assessing, referring, evaluating, coordinating, and reporting.

The remainder of this chapter is dedicated to operationalizing the school counselor's dual roles. In doing so, the specific functions and activities inherent in each unique role are described.

SCHOOL COUNSELOR: THE ROLE OF COUNSELOR

CACREP ensures the clinical competence of school counselors for the role of counselor by requiring successful articulation through eight core counseling competencies. CACREP also ensures the counselor's readiness for the specialty of school counseling by requiring a successful

A Special Breed: Roles and Functio

ASCA, in collaboration with the CACREP, the TSCI, and professioi counseling associations, has made great strides in defining contei porary school counseling functions, services, and practices. Unfort nately, vague school counselor roles and inconsistency across stati and school division continue to strangle the profession's progress.

The mighty reaction that resonated within the profession with th TSCI's switch to an academic-focused paradigm implied neglecting th counseling role of the school counselor (Guerra, 1998). Some equated this to a change in professional identity—a change that some fear ma result in a unilateral identification of the school counselor as educa tor versus counselor. This concern is justifiable and further supporte by the administrative thrust toward encouraging school counseloi via salary supplements to earn the NBPTS national school counsel certification not afforded to those who earn the NBCC national scho counselor certification (discussed in chapter 1).

This book promotes the dual roles of educator and counselor, unde standing that our primary role is one of counselor, but that it is the ro of educator that makes us a special breed. It is the educator role th sets us apart from other counseling specialties. This chapter provide conceptualization and operationalization of these roles in the context a comprehensive school counseling program that attends to the whi child and adolescent.

Defining and framing school counselor functions in relation these dual roles provides a conceptually sound structure from wh to operationalize and authenticate the roles of the contemporary sch matriculation through school counseling specialty competencies. These competencies are outlined in chapter 1. These competencies prepare school counselors as both counselors and educators.

School counselors fulfilling the role of educator are not abandoning the personal, social, and emotional needs of students. Likewise, school counselors fulfilling the role of counselor are not abandoning the academic needs of students. The school counselor as educator, although focused on promoting academic achievement, has a distinct, but mutually supporting role as counselor attending to the holistic needs of students.

School counselors who believe it is futile to address the academic needs of students in the midst of personal, social, and physical challenges are likely perpetuating achievement gaps and inequitable access to educational opportunities. The fruits of academic-focused school counseling are enjoyed by all students. The academic-focused school counselor fully understands how personal, social, emotional, and physical development affects learning and designs prevention and intervention programs accordingly.

The systems-focus in the new era of school counseling, does not disregard individual counseling. Pizza dates back to the sixteenth century—a consistently respected food in this ever-changing world! Like pizza, individual counseling is a mainstay in school counseling.

School counselors are steadfast in addressing the individual holistic needs of students using individual counseling as a core responsive services delivery component of a comprehensive school counseling program (ASCA, 2012). The issue has been that the traditional mental health model has created an overreliance on individual counseling—a diet of nothing but pizza to the neglect of essential other food groups! This overreliance on individual counseling is inadequate and unjustifiable in this new era of systems-focused, direct and indirect services delivery.

Mental health models conceptualize social–emotional functioning as ends in themselves. This explains in part why some K–12 students are in individual school counseling "forever" and why school counseling goals from a mental health perspective are vague and tangential to an academic success and learning focus (Eschenauer & Hayes, 2005, p. 245).

For this reason, school counseling alone is not in the best interest of children and adolescents experiencing severe, persistent, and progressive issues. Additionally, to provide ongoing counseling sessions with students whose issues cannot be sufficiently addressed within the scope of school counseling and within the expertise of the school counselor is in violation of professional ethical guidelines. School counselors can best meet the specific mental health needs of these students through a collaborative model that recognizes when students' needs require more specialized skills.

Consider ants. Yes, you read correctly, I said *ants*. Our airlines looked to ants to optimize seating processes due to the astounding efficiency of the ant collective. Alone, ants are not nearly as efficient as the collective. Each ant is born with specific traits, which are strategically applied when that expertise is needed to benefit and ensure survival of the species.

In the spirit of the ant, school counselors work with other stakeholders to provide optimal and specialized services that place the safety and well-being of children first. School counselors may involve the school psychologist, school social worker, child study team, school nurse, and special education teachers. School counselors may provide parents with community resources that list but do not specifically endorse any one entity, such as specialized counselors, psychological and psychiatric services, social services, child care services, community services boards, spiritual and religious agencies, and support groups.

The new era for school counseling emphasizes collaboration, underscoring the need to make appropriate counseling referrals to meet the complex mental health needs of students. School counselors can help to reduce and even prevent the horrific acts of school violence demonstrated at Columbine, Virginia Tech, and other schools across the nation by remaining diligent in our efforts to identify and encourage familial support and make appropriate referrals for troubled students. Once appropriate referrals are in place, school counselors can implement brief interventions and consult with teachers and parents to provide strategies for implementation at home and in the classroom.

Response to Intervention and Positive Behavioral Support

Although originally conceptualized for students with disabilities, this next century leans heavily on Response to Intervention (RTI) and Positive Behavioral and Support Interventions (PBSI) to ensure early identification and intervention for struggling students. RTI and PBSI aid in mediating problematic behaviors, improving academic achievement, reducing school drop-out, and creating environments optimal to teaching and learning for all students.

As responsive services, RTI and PBSI are data-driven (e.g., discipline records, attendance reports, test scores, course enrollment patterns, special education placement patterns, gifted program placement patterns, graduation rates, college entrance records) and applied based on need. The core belief of these behavior systems is that some students need more intense or individualized instruction in order to be successful learners.

RTI and PBSI services are as unique as the students, varying in type, intensity, and duration based on level of need and progress toward established educational, career, and personal-social goals. Services may include:

- Dropout prevention and mediating attendance issues
- Decision making and goal setting
- Counseling and behavioral support
- Referral
- Career planning and assessment
- Parenting skills
- Transitioning

School counselors use a multitier approach to align the comprehensive school counseling program with the RTI and PBSI systematically applied processes, and use educational and behavioral data to monitor student progress (Schellenberg, 2012). Table 3.1 demonstrates this alignment and the school counselor's responsibility in the RTI process (ASCA Position Statement, Response to Intervention, 2008).

Strengths-based Counseling

Common school counseling responsive services include fostering optimism, cognitive restructuring, problem solving, strengths-based counseling, and promoting developmental assets. School counselors assist students in identifying support systems and unique personal attributes to strengthen protective factors and enhance resilience.

Table 3.1. Response to Intervention in a Comprehensive School Counseling Program

RTI Process	Role of the Professional School Counselor
Tier 1: Universal Core Instructional Interventions: All Students, Preventative and Proactive	1. Standards and Competencies (Foundation) 2. Guidance Curriculum (Delivery System) 3. Individual Student Planning (Delivery) 4. Curriculum Action Plan (Management) 5. Curriculum Results Report (Accountability)

Tier 2:
 	
Supplemental/Strategic Interventions: Students at Some Risk
	1. Standards and Competencies (Foundation)
	2. Individual Student Planning (Delivery)
	  a. Small-group appraisal
	  b. Small-group advisement
	3. Responsive Services (Delivery)
	  a. Consultation
	  b. Individual counseling
	  c. Small group counseling
	4. Closing the Gap Action Plan (Management)
	5. Closing the Gap Results Report (Accountability)

Tier 3:
 	
Intensive, Individual Interventions: Students at High Risk
	1. Standards and Competencies (Foundation)
	2. Responsive Services (Delivery)
	  a. Consultation
	  b. Individual counseling
	  c. Small group counseling
	  d. Referral to school or community services
	3. Closing the Gap Action Plan (Management)
	4. Closing the Gap Results Report (Accountability)

Adapted from ASCA Position Statement, Response to Intervention, 2008.

Strengths-based counseling interventions that place responsibility for success within the student are educational, empowering, and help develop coping skills that can be accessed into adulthood. Strengths-based counseling is an emerging positive psychology that accesses inherent strengths to identify student resources and supports for addressing the problem. The strengths-based approach emphasizes the importance of protective factors in combating risk factors and enhancing resilience. Current and past successes are considered in addressing future challenges. The approach embraces the philosophy that treatment is not just about fixing what is broken, but nurturing what is best within ourselves (Seligman, 2004).

School counselors use strengths-based counseling to build on students' unique assets, empowering, instilling hope, and strengthening resilience. Lists of development assets for early childhood, middle childhood, and adolescence are made available by the Search Institute (2007) at www.search-institute.org/developmental-assets/lists. Each list depicts forty developmental assets considered to be building blocks for healthy development. The following eight categories are included in the lists:

- Support
- Empowerment
- Boundaries and Expectations
- Constructive Use of Time
- Commitment to Learning
- Positive Values
- Social Competencies
- Positive Identity

The Invisible Student

There is also a clarion call in the new era to ensure that we identify and provide services to the "invisible mass of students" by way of broadening our conceptualization of responsive services (Sink, 2011, p. ii). Invisible students are those that appear on the surface to be doing just fine with average grades and no discipline—the students that come and go, making no waves and blending in with the crowd. However, the absence of waves could indicate a silent drowning and much lost potential for students, families, schools, communities, and our society. This is an unfamiliar focus for school counselors. Although, services are provided to all students as part of a comprehensive school counseling program, focused attention has been given to underachieving, special needs, at-risk, and advanced-functioning students. For the most part, the invisible student appears to have escaped our radar until now.

Strategies for identifying this historically underserved population are needed. The creation and revisiting of academic and career plans is one avenue to detecting the invisible student. Individual planning is another way to identify the invisible student as long as the school counselor meets with every student. Also, delivering career and academic core school counseling curriculum lessons in required high school courses such as personal finance or economics would allow students to be exposed to the curriculum during their matriculation through high school.

This is a promising approach to identifying those who may not have postsecondary plans (Schellenberg, Pritchard, & Szapkiw, n.d.).

The relationship between academic success and personal, emotional, social, and physical well-being is a door that swings both ways. As such, it is important for school counselors to encourage students faced with mental health–related issues and physical challenges to believe in their ability to change, grow, and overcome challenges. School counselors encourage impaired students to embrace academics as an avenue to a promising, self-directed future. Academic-focused channeling can be therapeutic, motivational, and build competencies, self-esteem, and psychological resilience—epitomizing the specialty of school counseling. Challenge can be our greatest asset, pushing us onward and upward. Standards blending, discussed later in this chapter, exploits this reciprocal relationship for total student development.

In addition to responsive services, school counselors demonstrate a heightened emphasis on being proactive in anticipating and meeting the mental health needs of students. Therefore, in addition to programs and lessons designed to meet the unique needs of a school population or specific classrooms, school counselors engage in purposeful programming designed to remove formidable personal, social, and emotional barriers to academic achievement.

Spiritual and Religious Development

A topic once taboo in our schools is emerging in this new era of school counseling in order to ethically meet the culturally diverse developmental and holistic needs of students. Spiritual/religious development is a critical aspect of human development, a cultural agent, and a natural component for exploration in the counseling process that significantly impacts the student's worldview and the counseling relationship (Ingersoll & Bauer, 2004; Rayburn, 2004; Schellenberg, 2012). How can we study Austrian folk dancing and disregard the waltz?

Section A.1 of ASCA's *Ethical Standards for School Counselors* (2010) states that school counselors "respect students' values, beliefs, and cultural background and do not impose school counselor's personal values on students or their families." The ASCA Ethical Standards Preamble and Section E.2.c, too, state that the school counselor "acquires educational, consultation and training experiences to improve awareness, knowledge, skills and effectiveness in working with, advocating for, and affirming all students from diverse populations including spiritual/religious identity and appearance." However, the ASCA School Counselor Competencies (2012) and ASCA Position Statements do not offer guidance as to how school counselors might go about effectively meeting the spiritual/religious needs of students.

Uncertain as to how to appropriately address the sensitive topic of spirituality and religion and to address the topic in a manner that would be considered by parents, students, and administrators to be ethical, professional, and legal, school counselors have for the most part elected to avoid the topic. In an effort to promote communications around this crucial topic and to provide needed guidance, ASCA committed an entire special issue in the 2004 journal, *Professional School Counseling* (PSC), to addressing the spiritual/religious development of students as part of a comprehensive school counseling program.

Much like building multicultural competence, building the competence needed to work with students who hold diverse spiritual and religious beliefs begins with identifying personal biases and committing to learning more about various spiritual and religious practices. Working within the worldviews of students necessitates an understanding of how religious/spiritual beliefs impact personal-social, academic, and career decisions.

When considering curriculum development for the school counseling program, allow your guiding philosophy to be teaching versus preaching (Wolf, 2004). That is, objectively educate about spirituality and religion by (1) being descriptive and unbiased in the information presented; (2) teaching respect and appreciation of diversity; and (3) introducing literature or current events for class/group discussion that involve spirituality, religion, personal beliefs, and values (Wolf, 2004). As Wolf points out, discussing issues related to spirituality are both constitutional and ethical in accordance with the First Amendment of the Constitution and the ASCA Code of Ethics, respectively.

In part, the key to maintaining objectivity while teaching on topics related to spirituality and religion begins with an understanding of the differences between spirituality and religion. Religion is an organized practice that generally involves specific beliefs, ritualized worship, and an establishment such as a church, while spirituality is generally broader, unstructured, and focused on the individual's essence of being in relation to nature and the universe, and may include religion (Schellenberg, 2012).

In addition to spiritual/religious sensitivity in individual and group counseling and school counseling core curriculum development, school counselors might also consider participating in student-initiated spiritual and religious events such as the annual "See You at the Pole" prayer meeting. Section 9524 of the Elementary and Secondary Education Act (ESEA) constitutionally protects prayer in public schools (U.S. Department of Education, 2003) and school counselors who explore issues of spirituality with students are engaging in both ethically responsible and culturally competent counseling practices (Schellenberg, 2012).

To offer school counselors guidelines for professional practice, the following Spiritual and Religious Competencies for School Counselors and approaches and strategies for meeting the spiritual and religious needs of students are provided (Kimbel & Schellenberg, n.d.). The Spiritual and Religious Competencies for School Counselors includes twenty competencies within five domains and are grounded in school counseling research and literature as well as professional standards and ethical codes. The first four domains of the Spiritual and Religious Competencies for School Counselors are adapted from the culture and worldview, counselor self-awareness, human and spiritual development, and assessment domains of the Competencies for Addressing Spiritual and Religious Issues in Counseling (ASERVIC, 2009). The final domain of the Spiritual and Religious Competencies for School Counselors aligns with the delivery component of the ASCA National Model (2012), as school counselors spend a significant amount of time addressing this component by providing direct and indirect services compared to responsibilities related to the other three components (i.e., foundation, management, and accountability). The Spiritual and Religous Competencies for School Counselors are listed in Table 3.2.

The delivery component of the ASCA National Model accounts for 80 percent of the school counselor's use of time (ASCA, 2012). For this reason, approaches and techniques for practical application in the

Table 3.2.   The Spiritual and Religous Competencies for School Counselors

I. Spirituality/Religion and Worldview
   A. Professional school counselor possess a general understanding of atheism and agnosticism, as well as the similarities and differences of spirituality and religion, and how each construct may or may not be viewed by various stakeholders.
   B. Professional school counselors understand that spirituality, religion, atheism, agnosticism, characteristics, and experiences related to diverse belief systems impact students' personal, social, academic, and career development, personal identity development, worldview, and behavior.
   C. Professional school counselors have a basic knowledge of prevailing spiritual/religious denominations around the world and view student belief systems as developmental and cultural dimensions of students' lives.

II. School Counselor Self-Awareness
   A. Professional school counselors identify and explore their own spiritual/religious belief system and are aware of personal biases.
   B. Professional school counselors recognize how their own belief system and potential biases may impact the counselor–student relationship and counseling process.

III. Spiritual and Religious Development
   A. Professional school counselors view spirituality/religion as a natural dimension of human development that has potential to affect students of all ages.
   B. Professional school counselors possess a basic knowledge about models of spiritual and religious/faith development.
   C. Professional school counselors are knowledgeable of common belief system issues that arise in school-age populations at specific developmental levels.

IV. Assessment
   A. Professional school counselors are sensitive to spiritual/religious biases that may exist in formal and informal student assessment instruments or practices.
   B. Professional school counselors consider students' religious/spiritual beliefs and values during formal and informal student assessments.

V. Delivery of Student Services
   A. Direct Student Services
      1. School Counseling Core Curriculum
         a. Professional school counselors implement a comprehensive school counseling program that attends to the holistic needs of students by including practices that involve the diverse belief systems of the students.
         b Professional school counselors integrate spirituality/religion into classroom instruction and group activities in an objective manner.
         c. Professional school counselors allow opportunities during classroom instruction and group activities for sharing of all spiritual/religious beliefs and values (e.g., spirituality, religion, atheism, agnosticism).
      2. Individual Student Planning
         a. Professional school counselors understand how spiritual/religious beliefs and values impact student goals and decision-making, with regard to education and training as well as post-secondary career choices, and work within that belief system when advising and conducting student appraisal.
         b. Professional school counselors encourage exploration of spiritual/religious beliefs and values that impact goals-setting, education, and post-secondary planning and aid students in planning activities that align with their belief system.

3. Responsive Services
   a. Professional school counselors understand that spirituality/religion may be a powerful resource for building resilience and improving mental health.
   b. Professional school counselors provide individual counseling and crisis response services that provide students with an avenue for expression of values and belief systems and opportunities for exploration of issues related to students' belief systems.
B. Indirect Student Services
   1. Referrals
      a. Professional school counselors provide students and parents with resources that accommodate diverse belief systems (e.g., spirituality, religion, atheism, agnosticism) when referrals are warranted.
   2. Consultation
      a. Professional school counselors consult with stakeholders to solicit information, resources, and services that meet students' spiritual/religious development needs.
   3. Collaboration
      a. Professional school counselors serve on committees and team with stakeholders to cultivate safe and welcoming school climates for diverse spiritual and religious belief systems as well as conduct parent workshops on topics that teach to the developmental and cultural aspects of spirituality/religion in an impartial manner.

delivery of direct and indirect student services for Domain V of the Spiritual and Religious Competencies for School Counselors are suggested below.

School Counseling Core Curriculum

- Make use of spiritual/religious documents and books, including religious or "holy" books, during classroom instruction to teach civic values, virtues, and moral conduct.
- Explore with students ways in which they can meet goals and reach potential with good values, virtues, and moral conduct.
- Include religious and spiritual careers as options during career exploration curriculum delivery.
- Teach spiritual/religious beliefs and associated holidays during curriculum delivery.
- Implement school-wide programs that promote peer interactions, an appreciation of differences, and a climate where the peaceful resolve of problems are encouraged (e.g., peer mediation, conflict resolution, peer transition, new student orientation, tutoring).
- Engage students in developmentally appropriate discussions about current news and world reports and the role of moral conduct with regard to the events presented.
- Hang a poster in the school counseling office with a multitude of spiritual systems and religions represented.

Individual Student Planning

- Include volunteer work at food banks and homeless shelters in academic and career plans.
- Provide students with a list of community service agencies that include spiritual/religious organizations and activities.

Responsive Services

- Make use of bibliotherapy to illustrate exemplary moral behavior.
- Have students engage in role plays that are rich in opportunities to develop empathy, demonstrate respect for others, and to work through issues laden with spiritual/religious themes.
- Explore case studies to encourage reflection and reasoning as well as to highlight ways in which the case might be resolved using moral decision making and positive social interactions.

Referrals
- Develop a list of community resources for students/parents for career (e.g., employment, interest inventory Web sites) and academic support (e.g., tutoring, test preparation), as well as intervention for mental health issues (e.g., suicide ideation, eating disorders, depression). Include common spiritual and religious institutions and the services provided.
- Create comprehensive lists of common spiritual and religious belief systems and inform parents that you have such resources available.

Collaboration and Consultation
- Team with teachers to sponsor student-led spiritual/religious clubs.
- Team with teachers to conduct school-wide character education activities and recognitions, including morning announcements that emphasize a monthly virtue (e.g., perseverance, courage, truthfulness, kindness, patience, hope, humility).
- Partner with teachers to attend student-sponsored events before/after school such as the annual "See You at the Pole" meeting to model the importance placed on religious/spiritual values and beliefs in schools and communities.
- Conduct parent workshops on parenting styles and enlist objective research that speaks to the introduction of values and beliefs in relation to early child development and well-being.
- Conduct parent/teacher workshops on the impact of belief and values systems in relation to school violence and school climate as presented in the research (e.g., examine belief and value systems of differing countries and the prevalence of school violence).
- Partner with parents, teachers, and the community to coordinate stomp out violence activities that foster awareness and promote peaceable schools.
- Team with teachers and administrators to develop school mottos that revolve around the fair and equal treatment of all people and appreciation of differences.
- Work with parents and community agencies to coordinate an annual outdoor around the world day whereby all countries are represented, highlighting customs that include cuisine, clothing, spiritual and religious beliefs, and more.

Peer Programming

Students helping students is one of a school counselor's most valuable resources. Research to support the positive outcomes of peer-to-peer support programs is well documented (Whiston et al., 2011). Peer helping programs are also encouraged by ASCA with ethical guidelines established to ensure that student welfare is safeguarded, emphasizing the importance of proper training and supervision of peer helpers by school counselors (ASCA, 2010).

Peer-to-peer programs might include transition buddies, orientation programs, peer tutoring, and peer mediation. Chapter 4 provides an effective example of a school-wide peer mediation program and evaluation that identifies, targets, and reduces school violence, an obstacle to academic achievement and the personal, social, and emotional well-being of students (Schellenberg, Parks-Savage, & Rehfuss, 2007). The program studied establishes the need for school-wide peer mediation programs and reveals the link between peer mediation programs and academic achievement. The study documents research and literature that emphasize the detrimental effects of aggressive student interactions on the school's culture, learning environment, and academic productivity.

Proactive Change Agents

Proactive approaches to meeting the needs of students may require that school counselors position themselves in ways that increase visibility, which aids in enhancing school climate; fostering relationships with students, parents, teachers, and principals; and identifying at risk students (i.e., withdrawn, flat affect, socially inept, overly aggressive, visibly distressed). For example, school counselors may greet students in main hallways prior to the start of morning classes and at the end of the school day. School counselors might consider frequent visits to the cafeteria to give out bookmarks that contain useful information such as study and test-taking tips, important dates, names of school counselors, counseling department services and Web site, and career exploration resources and access codes. In addition, promoting the open-door policy, conveying an approachable demeanor, and maintaining a welcoming office (e.g., chair facing the door vs. back to the door) encourages interaction.

Many adults and students who experience distress do not actively seek out support (Auger, 2004). In addition, many stakeholders simply cannot find the time to make an appointment to meet with the school counselor. As such, it is important that school counselors be creative in getting meaningful information to stakeholders for sound decision making and problem solving. Information and resources might include crises response, support programs, parenting programs, tutoring contacts, substance use/abuse, eating disorders, counseling services available to students, study skills, test-taking strategies, organizational and time management skills, problem solving and conflict resolution, communication skills, and information that describes what to look for in determining the need for counseling services.

Establishing or tapping into a school-based Parent-Teacher-Student Resource Center (PTSRC) as an avenue for information dissemination is essential to meeting the needs of all stakeholders. PTSRCs are efficient mediums for promoting student development in a way that accommodates diverse schedules. The PTSRC is also an excellent way to get parents involved.

As Moles (1993) pointed out, there are many parents who want very much to get involved in the local school community but for a variety of reasons do not step forward. Extend an invitation to parents and be specific about the assistance and hours for which they are being recruited— watch what happens!

Parent volunteers are often an untapped resource in schools where human resources are generally limited. Parent volunteers can oversee daily PTSRC operations, providing assistance and direction to stakeholders seeking specific information, coordinating requests for information, and maintaining informational flow.

Web sites are another cost-effective and efficient medium for making resources available to stakeholders. Web sites communicate information in a broad and expedient manner so as to meet the immediate needs of stakeholders. Information and resources listed on school counseling Web sites can enhance student development and well-being and support healthy schools, homes, and communities.

School counselors are dogmatic in seeking to meet the mental health needs of students. By applying these constructs in this new era, school counselors expand services and promote a more proactive and collaborative approach to meeting students' personal, social, emotional, and physical needs. New era practices necessitate that school counselors exercise the counselor role in relation to fulfilling the educator role—the role that sets counseling in the schools apart from other counseling specialties and defines our profession.

SCHOOL COUNSELOR: THE ROLE OF EDUCATOR

Education and training that distinguishes the school counselor as an educator involves pre-K–12 program design and delivery, classroom instruction, theories of learning, child and adolescent development, standardized testing and assessment, use of technology, behavioral theory, disability and exceptional behavior, identification of student competencies and ways to achieve academic competency, identification and removal of barriers to academic achievement, developing effective learning environments, needs assessment, and educational program evaluation. Because fulfillment of the role of educator involves instruction, a few states still require a teaching background in order to become a school counselor. Therefore, it is important that this book speak to the research in this area of continued debate, which was deepened with the NBPTS's establishment of an advanced voluntary certification for school counselors (discussed in chapter 1).

Research has examined the question of whether or not school counselors should be teachers prior to becoming school counselors. These studies indicate that school administrators and school counselor supervisors deem school counselors without teaching experience to be as effective as those with teaching experience. Unexpectedly, in some cases the majority of school counselors without teaching experience were found to be more effective in their overall performance than those with teaching experience (Beale, 1995; Dilley, Foster, & Bowers, 1973; Olson & Allen, 1993).

One landmark study conducted during the crux of the debate provides evidence that having served as a teacher results in a multitude of poor counseling habits (Arbuckle, 1961). The implications of this study are significant, indicating a need for counselor educators to work closely with former teachers to extinguish most of what they had learned as teachers in order to become effective school counselors.

Arbuckle's (1961) findings are further supported in a more recent study of the personal and professional adjustments of school counseling interns with and without teaching experience. The study conducted by Peterson, Goodman, Keller, and McCauley (2004) indicated that former teachers faced unique challenges that threatened a successful transition into the school counseling profession.

Although it appears to have been established that teaching experience does not equal effective school counseling, there is general agreement that instructional skills are helpful in a profession that is expected to provide instruction. Therefore, counselor educators are diligent in their efforts to ensure the instructional competency of preservice school counselors in course curriculum and in the practice setting during counselor education programs.

In addition to the formal course work noted earlier in this chapter, counselor educators require demonstration of instructional competencies with diverse populations during classroom experiential learning activities and internships. Also, preservice school counselors are required to demonstrate knowledge of the pre-K–12 curriculum and engage in practicum and internship experiences throughout the counselor education program. Therefore, preservice school counselors have multiple opportunities to enhance their knowledge of curriculum development, collaborate with teachers, and to develop classroom management and instructional skills while also gaining a familiarity with the school setting.

Although, counselor education programs prepare school counselors for their role of educator, heightened emphasis on aligning school counseling activities with academic achievement accentuates the need to optimize the instructional competency and classroom management skills of school counselors. Therefore, supplementary school counselor training is suggested in instructional strategies, academic achievement, learning theory, multiple intelligences, and classroom management.

School counselors can increase their skills in the areas noted above by taking related courses as electives during their counselor education programs. School counselors might also consider engaging in self-initiated learning such as job shadowing, interviewing, and dialoguing with currently practicing teachers and principals. Reviewing journal articles and participating in instructional planning, conferences, and workshops and are additional ways in which school counselors can build instructional competencies.

Instruction is but one function inherent in the school counselor's role of educator. School counselors as educators are also required to apply academic standards, interpret standardized testing score reports, engage in standardized testing programs, develop research-supported curriculum, and create and evaluate needs- and standards-based educational programs. School counselors as educators also work with teachers to modify the classroom climate for optimal learning and to develop academic contracts and schedules of reinforcement.

New era school counselors join hands more tightly with teachers and administrators to identify systemic areas of academic deficits and specific low-achieving student populations. School counselors tailor programming to target academic needs while simultaneously meeting the personal, social, and career development needs of students. School counselors identify the divergent needs of each grade level, each classroom, and specific students, to inform core school counseling curriculum content, individual student planning, and responsive services delivery.

STANDARDS BLENDING: ALIGNING SCHOOL COUNSELING WITH ACADEMIC ACHIEVEMENT

Leaders in education and school counseling agree that implementation of standards-based programs that align school counseling with academic achievement missions are considered best practices for school counselors. Alignment approaches are needed that provide school counselors with a direct path for increasing academic achievement and closing the achievement gap.

To date, alignment approaches that integrate academic standards and school counseling standards have been random, spur-of-the-moment, superfluous, and/or absent from school counseling programming. This chapter introduces standards blending as a specific and unified crosswalking approach for inclusion as a deliberate, inveterate, and integral component of a comprehensive school counseling program. ASCA School Counselor Competencies (2012) require the school counselor to crosswalk the ASCA Student Standards with other appropriate standards. The paragraphs that follow demonstrate how standards blending can be implemented and assimilated as a permanent programming strategy for universal academic achievement.

Standards blending is a systems-focused, integrative, and student-centered crosswalking approach that directly and overtly aligns school counseling programs with academic achievement missions. School counselors methodically identify and blend specific core academic standards with school counseling standards for integrated lessons that assist students in making connections to real life and across curricula. As a primary and anchored appendage to a comprehensive developmental school counseling program, standards blending is the embodiment of academic- and systems-focused practices.

Standards blending does not replace the counselor role of the school counselor nor was it meant as an approach to address every unique issue within a school. The approach requires the school counselor to make use of their skills as both educator and counselor, integrating both school counseling and core academic standards. This crosswalking method allows the school counselor to meet the career, academic, and personal-social development needs of students while demonstrating a direct impact of academic achievement.

School counselors may wish to blend all core academic standards with the school counseling standards to create the alignment. However, it is recommended that language arts and mathematics standards be the focus of standards blending because reading, writing, and arithmetic have always been basic to schooling and to building a solid foundation from which to learn other core subjects.

In addition, reinforcing language arts and mathematics standards assists schools in meeting the goal of reading and math proficiency by the 2013–2014 school year as set forth by No Child Left Behind and thereby the professional leadership of school counselors and administrators. The national mathematics standards (NCTM, 2000), standards for the English language arts (NCTE, 1996), and the national school counseling standards (Campbell & Dahir, 1997) are applied because individual states use these standards to create more specific local standards, making them applicable to educators across the nation.

The unrelenting call for accountability in educational practices and standards-based educational reform has heightened the importance of rigorous standards and research-based practices by underscoring their importance in establishing evidence-based practices. Standards blending is grounded in these nationally accepted standards that are influenced by research and knowledge in the field.

In addition to a sound standards base, perception, process, and outcome data are collected to assess the meaningfulness of standards blending. To date, several studies validate the effectiveness of standards blending for delivery of developmentally and culturally sensitive school counseling services (Schellenberg, 2007, Schellenberg & Grothaus, 2009, 2011; Schellenberg, Pritchard, & Szapkiw, n.d.). These studies depict the usefulness of standards blending for the delivery of core school counseling curriculum, individual student planning, and responsive services at both the elementary and secondary levels with varying populations (e.g, ethnicity, special needs, advanced functioning). Research in the application of standards blending has consistently resulted in improved academic performance in mathematics and language arts, as well as the personal-social and career development of students.

Standards blending promotes the application of differential instruction, assessing student needs, accommodating unique student learning profiles, and considering student readiness and interests in curriculum planning and delivery. In addition, standards blending promotes the multiple learning categories (i.e., cognitive, affective, and psychomotor) and six learning levels of Bloom's Taxonomy (Bloom, 1953): knowledge, comprehension, application, analysis, synthesis, evaluation. As a holistic and constructivist approach, standards blending is an instructional strategy that is compatible with brain-based learning.

Standards blending encourages students to draw upon previous knowledge, make connections, get involved, explore, discuss, discover, and personalize the content. This crosswalking approach is pragmatic, providing students with a method by which to improve comprehension by connecting curricula and visualizing the interrelationships of learning and real life. Students socially interact with the curriculum, fellow students, and teachers in small learning communities where information is processed and problems are examined, deconstructed, and resolved. Approaches such as these have been linked to the development of background knowledge, intrinsic interest, and higher-order intelligence, as well as greater academic achievement and a heightened motivation toward learning (Marzano, 2004; Sink, 2005; Vansteenkiste, Lens, & Deci, 2006).

Blending academic standards and school counseling standards requires a working knowledge of school counseling and academic standards and consultation with the classroom teacher to coordinate the pacing of lessons. Most schools offer pacing guides that outline the timing of classroom instruction that addresses specific academic standards.

Standards blending can be delivered as an indirect service, teaming and partnering with teachers and parents to teach the crosswalking approach for use in the regular education classroom with a variety of subjects or outside of school in daily parent–child interactions and activities. Curriculum that includes the standards blending approach to deliver direct student services generally includes the school counseling core curriculum and responsive services, namely classroom lessons and small group programs, respectively.

Consider the following case for illustration of the delivery of core school counseling curriculum in a classroom or small group session using standards blending. The lesson blends both eighth grade national school counseling standards and national mathematics and language arts core academic standards. Also, note the differential instructional components in the lesson's design and activities and the inclusion of the three domains and six levels of learning of Bloom's Taxonomy.

The school counselor is preparing to deliver core school counseling curriculum and/or a small group session to eighth grade students that addresses the school counseling standards and student competencies for career development as deemed appropriate to a comprehensive school counseling program and as indicated by a needs assessment conducted at the start of the school year. The school's academic pacing guide or eighth grade teacher indicates that the eighth grade English teachers are working on oral language development with the students in March, specifically interviewing techniques to gain information—or this was identified as a need for a specific group of students, in which case small group counseling may be conducted.

In addition to school counseling standards and competencies, the school counselor incorporates the language arts standards being addressed at that time. The lesson curriculum includes a discussion of the importance of researching different careers to locate, evaluate, and interpret career and educational information (school counseling career development competency). Informational interviews are defined and discussed to include students' thoughts and feelings associated with the career exploration process and conducting informational interviews. Students are asked to give examples of the value and different uses of informational interviews and how they compare to other methods used in the past for the collection of information. Students are asked to conduct an informational interview (language arts competency) for the purpose of career exploration (school counseling competency). Individually, students prepare ten relevant questions for the interview (language arts competency). Students role play the interview with the school counselor and each other, asking the questions they prepared (language arts competency) and noting the responses (language arts competency). Together the class evaluates the effectiveness of the interviews in learning more about career choices (language arts and school counseling competencies).

Math standards being addressed by teachers at the present time include estimations, data analysis and conjectures, and identifying the mean of a data set. Therefore, the school counselor requires that at least five questions involve proportions such as scaling questions (e.g., how would you rate your job satisfaction on a scale of one to ten?). Students are then required to represent scaled responses using a table or graph, and then analyze patterns, relationships, and similarities within their data set and differences between each other's data sets. Together the group develops inferences about their findings (language arts, mathematics, and school counseling competencies).

The school counselor closes the lesson with an appraisal of the informational interview specific to career exploration. Students also judge the applicability and usefulness of informational interviews in other areas of their personal, academic, and professional lives. Again, the school counselor assesses students' thoughts and feelings associated with the career exploration process and conducting informational interviews.

The eighth grade lesson noted above can also be tailored to meet the developmental and educational needs of high school students. This school counseling lesson or small group activity applied to ninth, tenth, eleventh, and twelfth grade students meets school counseling career development standards as well as language arts (e.g., communication skills and strategies, evaluating data, developing research skills, application of language skills) and mathematics standards (e.g., number and operations, measurement, data analysis and probability, developing and evaluating inferences and predictions based on data, mathematical communication, connections, and representation).

Closing the Achievement Gap with Standards Blending

The new era in school counseling continues its emphasis on closing the achievement gap. School counselors disaggregate data and identify existing subgroup discrepancies in areas related to achievement. School counselors are then challenged to design approaches that assist in closing such gaps in order to demonstrate adequate yearly progress.

National data have identified academic achievement gaps between low-income and minority students and their more affluent peers, students with disabilities and nondisabled students, and between males and females. Therefore, once school counselors, in collaboration with school administrators and teachers, have identified low-achieving subgroups in a particular school/district, research-supported and standards-based programming should be designed to aid in closing achievement gaps.

In this new era, school counselors are continuing to demonstrate practices that aid in closing the achievement gap when students who are considered part of the gap participate in programs that apply standards blending and result in increased academic achievement. For example, once identified, school counselors can design small-group curriculum to specifically target areas of academic weaknesses. While strengthening areas of academic deficits, school counselors simultaneously address personal, social, academic, and career-related issues using standards blending. These issues may be identified by research as generally problematic, that is, causing or correlating with poor

academic achievement, or by teachers, students, and parents as an identified need (i.e., self-esteem, social skills, problem solving, test-taking
anxiety). Identification of need by research and stakeholder is a powerful union for programming support.

Low-achieving students often experience multiple precipitating
issues and stressors that frequently go unrecognized and untreated,
placing these students at risk for school failure. Using standards blending, school counselors can address the mental health needs of these
students, building personal, social, and emotional well-being and resilience, while simultaneously and directly addressing targeted academic
needs.

For example, several students are referred to the school counselor due
to personal, social, and behavioral issues. The school counselor, through
consultation with the teacher(s) and/or a review of student records/
data, finds that some of the students are also having difficulty in
mastering specific academic standards. Investigation also reveals that
the students are considered to be in the achievement gap population.
Although the school counselor could blend the core academic standards currently being addressed in the classroom, standards blending
becomes a more powerful and precise technique for closing achievement gaps when programming specifically targets students in the gap
in areas of academic weakness.

Consider the following lesson for illustration of a small group that
provides students with both remediation and reinforcement in language
arts and mathematics in addition to social skills development by way
of standards blending. Again, note in the lesson's design differential
instruction strategies, and the inclusion of Bloom's three domains and
six levels of learning.

A teacher refers Topeka, a third grade student, to the school counselor for a social skills small-group intervention. Consultation with the
teacher and a review of Topeka's class work and formal assessments
reveal difficulty in math, particularly with number and number sense
such as the concepts of greater than, less than, and equal to; parts of
sets; and fractions. As a result of school counselor–teacher consultation, while defining, identifying, experiencing, and appraising the
concepts of sharing and fairness in the social skills group using role
plays and social skills scenarios (language arts and school counseling

competencies), the school counselor also addresses areas of weaknesses in mathematics.

The school counselor gives Topeka twenty social skills scenario cards and asks her to give herself and each student the same, or an equal, number of cards (mathematics competencies). After Topeka has passed out all the cards, the school counselor counts the cards in front of each of the four students and involves students in discussions that connect the concepts of sharing, fairness, sets, greater than, less than, and fractions. The cards, students, and role plays are manipulated in order to visualize the relationships, create predictions, and to assess the value of the language arts, mathematics, and social skills concepts presented.

The school counselor encourages storytelling (language arts, mathematics, and school counseling competencies) to relate learning to individual student experiences, needs, and relationships—to life—and to ensure students' understanding of the information presented. Throughout the group lessons, each student's academic areas of weakness are addressed using differential instruction based on specific core academic standards in the areas of weakness and identified learning styles.

The small group using standards blending presented above is designed to enhance total student development by targeting personal, social, and academic areas to meet the specific needs of each student in the group. The school counselor addresses multiple areas of language arts and social skills, while also providing students with remediation in targeted areas of mathematics. The school counselor also reinforces a variety of grade-level appropriate mathematical concepts for all students.

In addition to the benefits to students, standards blending encourages consulting and teaming with teachers. An atmosphere of collaboration with teachers to accomplish student academic achievement goals has the potential to enhance the teacher–school counselor relationship and strengthen universal achievement.

SUMMARY

Implementation of the school counselor's dual roles of educator and counselor and the functions inherent in each role are central to the continued growth and unification of the profession in this new era. The school counselor as counselor meets the personal, social, and emotional needs of students within the scope of school counseling. This requires collaboration with professionals within and outside of the school system and the involvement and support of school administrators. The school counselor as educator identifies and removes barriers to academic achievement and, moreover, directly impacts academic achievement through well-planned instructional programming and a working knowledge of academic standards.

The school counselor adeptly combines the roles of educator and counselor using standards blending as a crosswalking approach that integrates academic and school counseling standards. Standards blending can also be used as a strategy for closing the achievement gap. The school counselor applies differential instructional philosophies with the constructs of Bloom's Taxonomy for creating optimal and individualized curriculum and learning environments.

CHAPTER 4

Our Bread and Butter: Research and Program Evaluation

Chapter 2 discussed how school counselors identify best practices gleaned from research to support curriculum content and systemic services delivery. During program planning school counselors identify measurable objectives and assess the program's effectiveness toward meeting those objectives using process, perception, and outcome data. In this regard, school counselors are delivering empirically validated programs that are both data-driven and data-producing.

Program evaluation is a type of action, or applied, research that is the most widely used in schools. It is invaluable in the educational setting where true experiments are extremely difficult due to vast uncontrollable variables and the ethical concerns of randomly assigning children and adolescents to treatment conditions and control groups. Program evaluation is an essential competency, legislative mandate, and ethical responsibility inherent to the position of school counselor. School counselors are obligated to systematically collect and analyze data to ensure the continuous improvement of our programming and to determine the usefulness of our services in meeting the needs of stakeholders.

Section F.1.c of ASCA's (2010) *Ethical Standards for School Counselors* states that school counselors "conduct appropriate research and report findings in a manner consistent with acceptable educational and psychological research practice. School counselors advocate for the protection of individual students' identities when using data for research or program planning" (p. 6). Section D.1.g calls for school counselors to develop "a systematic evaluation process for comprehensive, developmental, standards-based school counseling programs" (ASCA, 2010, p. 4).

Often in school counseling circles just the mention of data elicits a fleeing response similar to the mass exodus of the monarch butterfly migration to Mexico. Nonetheless, as the tide of accountability is expected to rise in this next era so too will the demand for data. Routinely gathering, examining, and generating data may help us to overcome our aversion to data while demonstrating reflective and investigative practices. Facilitating empirically supported school counseling activities can forever change the direction of a student's life.

Research and program evaluation will deliver us from the shadows into the sunlight. These are empowering and powerful proactive strategies that are vital in order to

- identify practices that contribute to academic success and the personal-social and career development of students
- develop empirically supported curriculum
- engage in professional advocacy
- provide reliable consultation services
- make programming decisions
- enhance accountability
- shape policy in the schools and at the local, state, and federal levels
- inform and sustain the profession
- justify funding/resource allocations
- assess the value of programming and practices

It is important to understand that the analysis of data for program planning and program evaluation do not equal accountability, but precede it as means by which to demonstrate accountable professional practices. Accountability also includes prevention and intervention programming that is supported by standards and services that are professionally, developmentally, ethically, legally, and culturally sound and justifiable.

Program evaluation demonstrates evidence over effort and answers the more critical question: how are students different as a result of school counseling programs? It is important that program evaluation become an integral component of the school counseling program's research, review, and feedback structure. Research and program evaluation are the school counselor's bread and butter—it sustains us as a profession.

PROCESS, PERCEPTION, AND OUTCOME EVALUATION

The call for program evaluation in school counseling and for collaborative research conducted by practitioners and counselor educators is mounting. Research partnerships benefit both counselor educators and school counseling practitioners. Collaborative studies provide counselor educators with an opportunity to stay apprised of rapidly changing practice needs for the contemporary school setting and to become involved in applied research in the school setting. Research partnerships with counselor educators provide school counselors with the opportunity to stay abreast of major developments in school counselor preparation, to target professional development activities, and to develop program evaluation skills and comfort levels with data collection, analysis, and reporting.

Program evaluations that measure outcome, that is, the effectiveness of the program in achieving intended goals, are important to establish a causal link between school counseling programs and student change, particularly academic achievement. Outcome evaluations, sometimes referred to as summative evaluations or quantitative evaluations, seek to answer the significant question—did it work?

Program evaluations measure process, that is, program functioning, strengths, weaknesses, and the extent to which the program meets the expectations of and serves the target population. Process evaluations, also known as formative evaluations and qualitative evaluations, are useful for program decision making and program improvement. Process evaluations seek to answer such questions as these: How did it work? How or with what population did it work best?

School counselors are wise to consider conducting program evaluations that include both measures of process and outcome. Even when outcome measures are positive, additional program data might provide knowledge that can be used to strengthen program outcomes, uncover further needs and unexpected benefits of the program, and identify additional target populations.

PROXIMAL AND DISTAL EVALUATIONS

Proximal evaluation measures are those that take place immediately before and after the program or intervention. Proximal evaluations allow school counselors to establish correlations, and, in some cases, depending upon the strength of the research design a causal link between school counseling interventions and outcomes.

Distal measures, on the other hand, are generally measures taken over time. Distal measures alone do not definitively link school counseling programming to student change due to the great number of factors (i.e., extraneous variables) that impact student development over time (i.e., between phases of evaluation).

There has been some debate over the significance of proximal (immediate) versus distal (long-term) evaluation in linking school counseling services to what students know and can do as a result of the program. However, since school counselors are called to provide well-defined data that demonstrate enhanced academic achievement and total student development that is clearly a result of school counseling programming then proximal evaluations that collect perception, process, and outcome data are the professional zeitgeist. Proximal evaluation methods, then, are the priority and primarily used to establish correlation, if not causality. Distal evaluations are often used as a means of cross validation to further support or call into question proximal evaluation outcomes and to offer insights into program strengths and weaknesses for ongoing improvement (Schellenberg, 2012).

Over time, consistent program evaluation will aid school counselors in building a strong knowledge foundation from which to expand, enhance, and tailor procedures and programming to the specific needs of a school division. This knowledge structure will allow school counselors and administrators to make declarative statements about the contributions of school counseling and future directions for school counseling programming.

METHODOLOGY

Program evaluation is a type of field-based outcome study, or as mentioned previously a type of action or applied research. There are an infinite number of other types of outcome research designs that could be used to measure any number of research questions. Three of the most commonly used outcome research designs by school counselors in the school setting are nonexperimental, quasiexperimental, and true experimental (Erford, 2011; Schellenberg, 2012). In short, the true experimental design is the strongest for establishing cause and effect, using random sampling and control groups. The quasiexperimental design does not use random assignment and involves multiple groups or multiple measures. Nonexperimental designs are generally one time surveys and single observations and have the least value for determining cause and effect between and intervention and the outcome.

Pre- and post-program instruments are the most widely used method of program evaluation. Methods may include behavioral observations, rating scales, student portfolios, and curriculum content instruments containing forced-choice items (e.g., multiple choice, true/false, Likert scale) for quantitative analysis.

Program evaluations that use triangulation (i.e., the incorporation of multiple sources of data) strengthen confidence in observed changes. For the same reason, statistical analysis is encouraged using paired sample t-tests for pre- and post-program data in addition to descriptive statistics such as percentages, categories, counts, and frequencies. An analysis of variance (ANOVA) is suggested for analyzing multiple observations, but attention must be given to statistical assumptions when using an ANOVA and the MANOVA (multivariate analysis of variance).

The example below illustrates evaluation questions, data sources, and methods of data analysis of a comprehensive program evaluation conducted by a school counselor in collaboration with counselor educators (Schellenberg et al., 2007). The evaluation includes both proximal and distal outcomes, process and outcome measures, multiple observations, and triangulation.

REDUCING LEVELS OF ELEMENTARY SCHOOL VIOLENCE WITH PEER MEDIATION

EVALUATION QUESTIONS,* DATA SOURCES, METHODS OF DATA ANALYSIS

- Does student knowledge pertaining to conflict, conflict resolution, and mediation increase as a result of Peace Pal training?
- Data Source: Pre-post–training questionnaire developed from curriculum and administered prior to training, immediately following training, and three months later.
- Data Analysis: Repeated Measures 1x3 ANOVA.
- Do peer mediation sessions result in the successful resolution of student conflict?
- Data Source: Peer mediation session records over one academic year. Data Analysis: Percentages.
- Do the number of schoolwide out-of-school suspensions decrease with the implementation of the Peace Pal program?
- Data Source: Out-of-school suspension data over a five-year period. Data Analysis: Frequencies and percentages.
- Do disputing students who participate in peer mediation sessions view the sessions as valuable?
- Data Source: Peer mediation session records over one academic year. Data Analysis: Percentages.
- Do peer mediators perceive the Peace Pal program as valuable?
- Data Source: Process questions five years post-program. Data Analysis: Percentages and qualitative.

Evaluation questions were derived from the goal and objectives of the program.

Adapted from Schellenberg et al., 2007.

ETHICAL AND LEGAL CONSIDERATIONS

It is important for school counselors to consider the ethical and legal issues associated with conducting research in the schools. Issues to consider include obtaining parental and student informed consent, confidentiality of assessment data, culture and gender bias in the selection of
measures, withholding treatment, and in the treatment of all students in
experimental groups. In addition to a review of the ACA's *Code of Ethics and Standards of Practice* (2005) and ASCA's *Ethical Standards
for School Counselors* (2010), the following resources are beneficial
when conducting studies in the public school setting: "Competencies
in Assessment and Evaluation for School Counselors" (Association for
Assessment in Counseling and Education, 1998); *Counseling and Educational Research* (Houser, 1998); *Guiding Principles for Evaluators*
(American Evaluation Association, 1994); and *Program Evaluation:
Methods and Case Studies* (Posavac & Carey, 2003).

SUMMARY

It is the school counselor's professional and ethical responsibility to
demonstrate, document, and promote accountable practices using research and program evaluation. Practitioner and educator-practitioner
research is needed that clearly depicts both the immediate and long-
term impact of school counseling prevention and intervention activities
on student development, in general, and on student academic achievement in particular.

Debate continues regarding the importance of proximal versus distal evaluations in establishing a stronger correlational, if not causal,
relationship between school counseling programming and student
outcomes. While outcome-based evaluations are the priority in school
counseling practices, process evaluations have value as well, suggest-
ing the application of a mixed-method approach. Regardless of the type
of research and program evaluation conducted, school counselors need
to be aware of the ethical and legal issues associated with conducting
research in the school setting.

CHAPTER 5

On Becoming the Quintessential New Era School Counselor

The journey to becoming the quintessential new era school counselor begins with rigorous preparation guided by standards and best practices. Formal education establishes a critical solid foundation. Much of what the new era school counselor learns takes place during practice through visionary leadership, continuous self-reflection, ongoing professional development, active counseling and school counseling association memberships, and networking with others in the profession.

COUNSELOR EDUCATOR

Counselor educators create and shape the attitude, knowledge, skills, and abilities that school counselors bring to the practice setting. Counselor educators use a variety of educational and instructional philosophies, models, and techniques so as to provide preservice school counselors with a broad repertoire of approaches and tools vital to practice in a setting that is changing at dizzying rates.

This text provides counselor educators with pragmatic tools and approaches for preparing school counselors to be proactive in anticipating academic- and systems-focused programming and accountable practices into the next century. When introducing preservice school counselors to the information and resources in this text, it is important to stress that the ultimate goal is to practice accountable programming on a daily basis—not once in a while. Like administrators, counselor educators understand that accountability has taken permanent residence in school counseling.

Meeting the challenges of contemporary school counseling necessitates that counselor educators teach to the realities of contemporary
school counseling practices. Teaching from an academic- and systems-
focused pedagogy that illustrates the practical needs of schools, current
trends and developments in school counseling and education, school
reform initiatives, and school administrator expectations, prepares preservice school counselors for the realities of practice.

PEDAGOGY

Due to historical adoption of the mental health–focused pedagogy
for school counseling, counselor educators are well-experienced and
adept in providing clinical instruction that stresses the application of
counseling theory and counseling techniques, particularly as it applies
to minors, as well as the legal and ethical considerations of counseling
practices in the school setting. Counselor educator expertise in this area
is indispensable to clinical competency and must continue in order for
the school counselor to practice skillfully in the role of counselor for
children and adolescents.

It is important, however, for counselor educators to ensure that preservice school counselors understand the scope of school counseling
practices, specifically with regard to providing mental health–related
services to students. Ensuring that preservice school counselors can
distinguish between appropriate and inappropriate services, and understand situations in which collaboration and referral within and outside
of the school are necessary, is vital to the development, well-being, and
safety of children.

Counselor educators, who introduce the national and state academic
content standards in addition to the school counseling standards, are
preparing preservice school counselors to meet the expectations of
school administrators, who seek out school counselors capable of
crosswalking curriculum to aid in the academic achievement mission.
Requiring preservice school counselors to apply both sets of standards,
differential instruction, and Bloom's constructs in the planning and
delivery of lessons provides opportunities to practice and build necessary skills in these areas. Having preservice school counselors apply

these strategies using diverse student populations, group topics, and group sizes reflects the realities of professional practice in a culturally pluralistic educational system.

Teaching standards blending as a fixed crosswalking appendage to comprehensive school counseling models such as the ASCA's *National Model* (2012), provides preservice school counselors with a solid foundation and framework from which to build an integrative, academic-focused program that school administrators can readily support. Standards blending is also an excellent approach for fulfilling CACREP foundations and contextual dimensions for school counseling program standards and the competency requirements for school counselors.

Readying the preservice school counselor for core school counseling curriculum delivery necessitates counselor educator encouragement toward education and training related to instruction. Encouraging (or requiring) preservice school counselor participation in instructional foundation courses also promotes a positive attitude toward academic-focused practices and the school counselor's role of educator. Counselor educators can guide preservice school counselors toward the selection of appropriate courses as part of their electives or supplemental training. Also, involving preservice school counselors in collaborative research projects with school counseling practitioners provides an applied means by which to develop instructional and teaching skills.

Counselor educators might also incorporate curriculum development, instructional strategies, and classroom management, as well as student assessment, achievement, and learning styles into school counseling courses and experiential learning. Strengthening preservice school counselor knowledge and skills in these instructional-related areas can aid in abolishing teaching requirements for school counselor licensure, discussed in chapter three, which continues in a few states.

Bridging New Era Theory and Practice

Bridging theory and practice requires an understanding of theory and practice. Counselor educators stay abreast of current school reform legislation and trends in education by visiting and shadowing in local school counseling programs from time-to-time and surveying local school counseling practitioners. Perusing research and literature that describes the strengths and shortcomings of school counseling practices and programming is an excellent way to strengthen counselor education programs and introduce preservice school counselors to the transformed roles and functions of school counseling in this new era.

Group dialogue and literature reviews pertaining to the issues that prompted the need for change in school counseling are essential to a thorough understanding of the needs of contemporary practice. Also essential are discussions about the importance of, and how to secure school administrator support with regard to implementing a comprehensive school counseling program that attends to the holistic needs of all students and promotes academic achievement. Doses of reality early in the program aid in establishing an understanding of professional practice in a dynamic climate defined by accelerated change.

For example, having school administrators from both the elementary and secondary levels serve as guest lecturers or engage in candid roundtable discussions in the classroom aids preservice school counselors in understanding the immediate needs of schools and role expectations of administrators. Engaging in experiential learning activities enhances knowledge of school environments, norms, policies, and procedures and increases the likelihood of successful academic-focused programming in practice.

As preservice school counselors begin to develop an understanding of the relationship between theory and practice, practical approaches and tools are necessary to guide the implementation of accountable academic- and systems-focused programming. Teaching students to use alignment approaches such as standards blending meets CACREP standards, the recommendations of ASCA, and school improvement initiatives.

CACREP underscores the importance of preparing preservice school counselors to meet the realities of contemporary practice that include increased diversity and advanced technology. The student-centered, integrative nature of standards blending coupled with differential instructional practices and Bloom's constructs is ideal for developing preservice school counselor knowledge and skills related to meeting the diverse needs of students and developing strategies for closing the achievement gap. Introducing preservice school counselors to the countless forms used in daily practice, including reporting tools such as the School Counseling Operational Plan for Effectiveness (SCOPE) and the School Counseling Operational Report of Effectiveness (SCORE) to document action plans, lesson plans, and results reports will aid students in understanding the steps involved in accountable programming (see chapter six).

School counseling interns who share crosswalking strategies, data reporting tools, and ethically and legally sound forms during internships promote a reciprocal relationship and accountability. Interns have the potential to permeate settings where the traditionalist mindset continues to prevail and crosswalking approaches and data reporting systems are absent or inadequate. These preservice school counselors, armed with a new era of tools and approaches can make great strides in affecting change in practice.

Research Collaboration

Collaborative research partnerships between counselor educators and school counseling practitioners are powerful alliances with the potential to improve educational and professional school counseling practices and student academic achievement. It is vital to the continued growth of our profession that counselor educators take advantage of every opportunity to actively engage in collaborative research that adds to the body of literature and supports academic- and systems-focused school counseling programs.

Research collaboration with practitioners also addresses the immediate need to train currently practicing school counselors in data collection, data analysis, results interpretation, and program evaluation methodology. School counselors who learn these essential skills through the research collaboration process are in a better position to continue engaging in evaluative studies that support the efficacy of contemporary programming. In turn, school counselors can provide counselor educators with access to the practice and research setting and an understanding of the unique and ever-changing needs of the school/division.

Collaborating on the publication of research outcomes aids in developing practitioner skills in scholarly publication, while also promoting the positive impact and value of school counseling services on academic achievement and total student development. Publication informs and benefits all stakeholders, demonstrating how theory drives practice and how practice, in turn, informs theory.

SCHOOL COUNSELOR

Changing the pedagogy in counselor education to reflect a new era of systems-focused practices is fundamental to aligning school counseling with the academic achievement mission of schools and to maturing our profession. However, unless these changes occur in practice, school counselors may risk losing their jobs. A professional survival mentality may be warranted, as some districts have already eliminated school counselor positions due to role confusion, role conflict, and role inconsistency in addition to a lack of data supporting the school counselor's value in creating positive outcomes for student career, personal-social, and academic development. The need to establish the profession as one that attends to the whole student and squarely contributes to academic achievement is gaining momentum.

Much work is ahead that requires a commitment to change. School counselors must take the road less traveled and partner with school administrators, apply approaches that directly and overtly align with academic development, create action plans and results reports, and share programming practices and outcomes. School counselors are urged to make use of technology as a vehicle to fortify accountability and professional advocacy efforts.

Change and engaging in unfamiliar practices creates internal struggle for many individuals. Stay positive and focused—struggle strengthens us and creates growth. And, although growth can be painful, somewhere in the struggle emerges a higher level of excellence, enthusiasm, and passion for the profession.

It is an exciting time to be a part of the school counseling profession as we strive to establish the school counselor as an indispensable member of the educational team. United in our efforts, a new era of progress and unprecedented maturity is imminent.

New Era Programming

Accepting the challenge to implement systemic change, meet the holistic needs of students, and raise academic achievement for all students with collaborative accountable programming requires (1) gaining leadership and support of school administrators, (2) establishing advisory committees, (3) assuming the roles of both counselor and educator, (4) collecting and examining data for needs-driven programming, (5) blending academic and school counseling standards, (6) developing research-supported curriculum, (7) conducting program evaluations, (8) using available technology, and (9) creating and disseminating action plans and results reports. Using the standards-blending approach, school counselors are no longer implying an alignment with academic achievement missions but demonstrating the alignment in an overt and direct manner. School counselors, who become accustomed to routinely applying standards blending as a permanent appendage to the comprehensive school counseling program are promoting lasting change in school counseling.

Keep in mind that standards blending can be extended beyond the classroom. School counselors can team with parents to identify a broad range of issues and topics of importance to parents and families (e.g., safety at home and in the community, chores, deployment, familial relationships). School counselors can hold small group workshops that teach parents how to blend their child's academic standards into personal-social topics discussed at home. Parents who engage in standards blending with their students are imparting important life skills while reinforcing academics in targeted areas.

Standards blending to a school counselor is like a blank canvas to an artist. Working with school administrators, parents, students, teachers, and data, the possibilities for affecting change, heightening academic achievement, closing the achievement gap, and enhancing total student development are limited only by the boundaries of the school counselor's creative mind. Do not hesitate to seek out ideas and feedback from stakeholders—harness the creative power of collective minds!

Documentation of program plans and outcomes is not benefiting anyone if the information stays in the closet. School counselors are encouraged to share action plans and results reports. The use of SCOPE and SCORE is encouraged to aid school counselor in navigating the often foreign waters of data management and outcome reporting. SCOPE and SCORE can be disseminated in seconds to efficiently communicate information to stakeholders that demonstrates how school counseling services are making a difference in the lives of children.

Transitioning with Technology

Technology broadens the school counselor's potential for professional advocacy. More than a billion people use the Internet for professional and personal reasons, making this information infrastructure a powerful and pervasive communication tool.

The Internet provides school counselors with a broad-reaching, practical, and proficient medium for communication with stakeholders. Mass communication is particularly important during this new era of maturity. School counselors need to inform stakeholders about the changing landscape of school counseling and how these changes improve services and strengthen the profession.

A review of literature (White, 2007) exposes the importance of school counselors becoming literate in information technology in order to meet the demands of this digital age. Van Horn and Myrick (2001) identified technology, particularly the Internet, as an important mechanism in determining the success of school counseling programs, yet many school counselors do not have a presence on the Web. Those school counselors with a presence on the Web are not generally using the site to inform stakeholders, reverse historical trends, and promote the contemporary practices of a renewed profession.

Departmental Web sites are useful in sharing the beliefs and practices of professional school counselors, informing important others about current trends and developments, including adoption of the term *school counselor* to replace *guidance counselor*. Web sites can also be used to shape perceptions and effect change in systems that have not adopted the new vision for school counseling.

School counseling programs become that much more meaningful and credible when stakeholders have an understanding of practices and programming and view the school counselor as a knowledgeable professional. Therefore, at the very least Web sites should communicate (1) school counselor roles and functions; (2) school counselor education, training, and credentials; (3) information regarding professional associations; (4) current trends and developments in the profession to include the ASCA model and the changed language; and (5) mission statements and program goals that clearly connect school counseling to the academic achievement mission of schools.

School counselors are encouraged to explore the plethora of computer technology applications. In addition to professional advocacy, advanced technology can be used by school counselors for the following: clinical supervision, group and individual consultation, conferencing, online mentoring and peer mediation, database sharing, research and professional development, information retrieval and dissemination, career development, prevention and intervention activities, and assistive devices and services for special-needs and diverse populations.

Professional Identity and Advocacy

Promoting a unified professional identity and engaging in professional advocacy requires staying abreast of the research and current trends and developments that impact school counseling practices. Remaining proficient in the profession involves reading professional journals and newsletters, maintaining professional association memberships, attending conferences, and networking with counseling professionals within and outside of the school setting to include counselor educators. School counselors use this information to enhance practices and to promote unified roles, functions, and the changed language of the profession.

Lifelong learning is essential in this young profession that is experiencing unprecedented change and rapid growth. Continuous professional development allows school counselors to astutely communicate with stakeholders and to effectively meet the needs of students with the continuous improvement of practices.

Clearly articulating the school counselor's dual roles and functions to stakeholders, primarily school administrators is important; however, let us not forget the familiar cliché—*actions speak louder than words*. Thus, modeling the changed language of our profession and consistently demonstrating how school counseling programs contribute to academic achievement and total student development is the most effective means of professional advocacy and establishing a professional identity for school counselors.

Teaming with other educators in the planning and delivery of services is another valuable means by which to advocate for the renewed profession that views collaboration as an endless resource. The school counselor actively seeks out opportunities to work with colleagues, teachers, counselor educators, administrators, and parents.

Standards blending provides an ideal opportunity for collaboration with classroom teachers, who genuinely appreciate the reinforcement of academic standards within and outside of the classroom. School counselors can team with resource teachers, such as art and music teachers, to provide creative and dramatic musicals and assemblies that involve students, include academic and school counseling standards, and can be presented to the entire student body. This is also a great way to get parents and the community involved in programming.

School counselors can also make a difference outside of the school building, which will positively affect practices inside of the school building. School counselors might consider attending and presenting at professional education and counseling conferences and in the community, joining or establishing a regional school counseling leadership team, joining professional associations, serving as an officer on professional associations or credentialing boards, and engaging in research collaboration with counselor educators.

School counselors might also consider presenting on contemporary and academic-focused school counseling topics at staff development meetings to an audience of school administrators. School administrators appreciate insight into the changes that are occurring in the school counseling profession. School administrators also value fresh ideas as to how those changes can enhance student achievement and contribute to school improvement.

School counselors know how school counseling makes a difference in the lives of children, but we have been negligent in demonstrating an overt alignment with, and direct impact on, academic achievement. We have also been lax in providing stakeholders with essential documentation that depicts accountable practices and positive program outcomes, which establishes the value of our profession. It is time to get off the sidelines and into the game—the clock is running and many are keeping score!

SCHOOL COUNSELOR SUPERVISOR

School counselor supervisors are in a unique position to represent the interests of both school administrators and school counselors. The traditional paradigm was somewhat problematic for the school counselor supervisor, who had some difficulty defining how the school counselor's roles and functions clearly contributed to academic achievement and aligned with the school's mission. The implied nature of contributions to student development, primarily academic achievement, has not been enough to fully secure support for school counseling programs.

The compatible interests and aligned missions of school administrators and today's school counselors provides enthusiastic school counselor supervisors with a new platform from which to promote change, professional identity, and a unified profession, as well as advocate on behalf of school counselors. School counselor supervisors also aid in the recruitment and selection of highly qualified school counselors. This calls for an understanding of that which constitutes a highly qualified school counselor prepared to keep the profession on the path to maturity. Counselor supervisors, too, ensure the continued preparation of school counselors by supporting and encouraging continuous professional development and advanced level credentialing.

Implementing School Counselor Roles and Functions

School counselor supervisors create school counselor job descriptions and performance evaluations to reflect the new vision school counselor's roles and functions at the elementary and secondary levels. School counselor supervisors and administrators can refer to the CACREP standards, ASCA national model, TSCI, state standards for school counseling programs, and this text for guidance in redefining school counselor duties and responsibilities.

Job descriptions and performance expectations identify the essential functions of school counselors at each educational level. This is particularly important for pertinent school counselor performance evaluation and for identifying job-related search criteria for school counselor recruitment and selection.

Selecting New Era School Counselors

Principals do not generally have a background or education in school counseling and may be unaware of the contemporary roles and functions of school counselors, yet they are often responsible for hiring school counselors. Therefore, it is imperative that school counselor supervisors provide guidance to school administrators in selecting well-prepared school counselors that understand the direction of the profession.

The level of guidance provided by the school counselor supervisor is largely dependent upon the size of the school and school district. Guidance may entail working closely with principals to provide selection criteria and standardized interview questions. Guidance might also require the supervisor's direct participation in the screening of applications and interviewing of prospective school counselor candidates.

Professional Development

This book provides school counselor supervisors with the information, approaches, and tools for fulfilling their administrative supervision role. However, fulfillment of the clinical supervision role requires graduate-level training in counseling and counselor supervision in addition to advanced state and national counselor credentials.

School counselor supervisors are urged to continue their education and professional development specific to counselor supervision, namely models of supervision specific to counseling. Understanding and developing the ability to apply models of counselor supervision is vital to the optimal functioning of the individual school counselor as well as the school counseling team.

In addition to education and progressive credentials, school counselor supervisors add to their credibility as an advanced level school counselor and effective leader by remaining actively involved in the profession. School counselor supervisors are expected to maintain professional association membership, present at conferences, publish in peer-reviewed journals, and collaborate with counselor educators.

When school counselors view the counselor supervisor as credible, they are more likely to be open to leadership and to actively seek out the supervisor for opportunities to develop higher-level knowledge and skills. In addition to credibility, the school counselor supervisor must be viewed as approachable, nonconfrontational, and nonjudgmental. An atmosphere that welcomes questions, views mistakes as an opportunity for growth, and demonstrates a team approach to obtaining answers is conducive to learning and optimal functioning. School counselors will seek answers from colleagues, which may or may not be correct in the absence of an approachable school counselor supervisor.

It is important for school counselor supervisors to accept that they cannot and will not know it all. While an approachable attitude and advanced education and counselor credentials are essential to optimal administrative and clinical competence, as well as effective leadership, having all the answers is not. Our ever-changing global workforce is exceedingly specialized. An effective leader is a resourceful visionary who consults with those most knowledgeable in a particular area and/ or program and engages in a needs-driven, team approach to decision making, process and program implementation, and systemic change.

Changing traditional ways of responding to student needs is particularly challenging for even the most adept school counselors. The reform-minded supervisor is a lifeline for school counselors who are not knowledgeable of or who are having difficulty implementing contemporary and academic-focused practices. Supervisors provide school counselors with administrative and clinical supervision as well as information, resources, tools, and approaches for implementing accountable, comprehensive school counseling programs that align with district and state academic achievement missions.

Encouraging the use of standards blending as part of the comprehensive school counseling program clearly aligns the program with the academic achievement mission of schools. Including SCOPE and SCORE as tools to be used by school counselors for developing accountable programs and documenting impact data provides counselor supervisors with advocacy instruments to share with school administrators.

School counselor supervisors model desired practices and provide professional development opportunities to school counselors for understanding and fulfilling their dual roles and functions. As newly acquired knowledge and skills are applied and the school counseling program begins to transform, so, too, does the individual school counselor, which may create unanticipated conflict and discomfort for some. It is important for school counseling supervisors to understand that in the midst of change even the most seasoned school counselors may experience many of the same thoughts and feelings of uncertainty and dependency of a beginning school counselor. School counselor supervisors, anticipating the struggle, foresee the stumbling, which they meet with encouragement, problem solving, and a focus on what is being learned while on the road to discovery.

Understanding developmental models of counselor supervision is extremely useful. It may be necessary to temporarily adjust levels of counselor supervision until the challenged school counselor regains perceptions of competence and stability as we enter into this new era of possibilities.

Meeting challenges with a positive attitude and a focus on a shared vision for school counseling may aid in reducing resistance while individuals and the system seek to reestablish homeostasis. Exhausting at times, the outcome is worth the journey.

SCHOOL ADMINISTRATOR

It has been a decade since implementation of a new vision for school counseling. Still, there is a dearth of commentary in the field on this major development with many school divisions continuing to go about business as usual. Several factors are contributing to this reluctance or inability to cede the traditional school counseling paradigm.

Some within the profession fear that the new paradigm direction threatens the status quo, and so remain shackled to traditional mental health– and individual-focused practices. Others simply prefer the comfort of complacency over change, while others recognize the need for change, but feel a lack of support toward change and a lack of practical processes, approaches, and tools for implementing change.

School administrators have not been fully informed, or have been misinformed, regarding the renewed profession. And, since the success of the school counseling program is inextricably tied to school administrator acceptance and stewardship, this text is designed to (1) serve as the communication conduit for understanding school counseling in this new era and the inherent dual roles and functions of the school counselor, (2) provide the impetus for the development of a symbiotic relationship between school administrators and school counselors, (3) promote the implementation of comprehensive school counseling programs that attend to the holistic development of students and focus on universal academic achievement, and (4) emphasize the importance of school counselor and school counselor supervisor selection and promotion practices in ensuring highly qualified school counseling teams driven by a shared vision.

School administrator leadership is the essential missing link to institutionalizing a comprehensive school counseling program that fully attends to the holistic needs of students—a laudable child-first goal. School administrators who support the implementation of comprehensive school counseling programs with an emphasis on holistic student development are ushering in a new era for school counseling and school systems.

SUPPORTING THE NEW ERA AND
A UNIFIED PROFESSIONAL IDENTITY

Over the years, school counselors have been assigned duties and responsibilities that are unrelated to school counseling due to inconsistent pedagogies in counselor education, role ambiguity, and a lack of accountability in professional practices. For example, many school counselors are maintaining student records, supervising study halls, serving as meeting secretaries, acting as teachers and substitute teachers and/or disciplinarians, operating attendance tables, and assisting the front office clerical staff. Studies show that assignment to noncounseling duties are taking up to 50 percent of school counselors' time (Burnham & Jackson, 2000) and are not cost efficient or an effective use of manpower (Hardesty & Dillard, 1994).

Instead, school counselors could be identifying low-achieving populations and developing programs designed to have a direct positive impact on closing achievement gaps. School counselors could also be applying systems-focused strategies to enhance student motivation to learn, attend school, and graduate. The school counselor's time would also be better spent collaborating with teachers to implement standards blending.

On the threshold of this exciting migration to a new era for school counseling, school administrators can expect to encounter resistance akin to challenging the big bang theory. Resistance is a hurdle to overcome and one that is not new to school administrators. School counselors and school counselor supervisors with an allegiance to the traditional paradigm are likely to challenge those who are plowing forward into the new era to a paradigm debate. Such a challenge is lamentable, but not unanticipated and met with analytic simplicity— academic-focused practices are recognized in the profession as an essential, pragmatic, and theoretically sound and in the best interest of all stakeholders.

Selecting New Era School Counselor Supervisors

School administrators are vicariously responsible for the actions and inactions of school counseling practitioners. As such, it is in the best interest of school administrators to look beyond the minimal competencies of master's degrees and mandatory licensure by states' departments of education when selecting school counselors and school counselor supervisors. As more school administrators base selection and promotion decisions on a preference for school counselors who hold advanced-level credentialing more school counseling practitioners will seek to obtain such credentials. ASCA offers information regarding the purpose, duties, responsibilities, and required and desired qualifications of a school counselor supervisor on their Web site listed in chapter 1. The need for at least one highly qualified school counselor supervisor in each school division who is qualified to provide both clinical and administrative supervision has been well-documented.

Well-qualified school counselor supervisor candidates have a track record of presentation, publication, and self-initiated professional development demonstrative of a passion for the profession. Active participation in the profession leads to a deeper knowledge and understanding of contemporary school counseling practices clearly demonstrated by the use of the contemporary language of the profession (e.g., school counselor versus guidance counselor). Highly qualified school counselor supervisors have the education, training, and credentials to provide both clinical and administrative supervision.

Potential school counselor supervisors hold the credentials of National Certified Counselor (NCC), National Certified School Counselor (NCSC), and Licensed Professional Counselor (LPC) indicative of optimal preparation as a professional school counselor and counselor.

Advanced voluntary credentials also demonstrate a commitment to professional development and a motivation toward professional advancement and skills improvement. Ideally, school counselor supervisors possess a doctoral degree in counselor supervision.

Having administrative and clinical expertise are essential to school counselor leadership and to directing the school counselor's dual roles of educator and counselor. School counselors who have access to clinical supervision experience enhanced counseling skills, effectiveness, and accountability; increased confidence and competence; and are more motivated toward professional development (Agnew, Vaught, Getz, & Fortune, 2000; Crutchfield & Borders, 1997). Clinical supervision also assists school counselors in enhancing their counseling and decision-making skills for more effective management of routinely complex cases and for ensuring optimal student development and a safe school environment.

Responding adequately to student needs that may involve severe depression, homicide and suicide ideation, substance abuse, school violence, child abuse, and pregnancy requires that school counseling practitioners apply proficient clinical skills and knowledge of the legal and ethical implications of their actions or inactions. For these reasons, school counselors have expressed their desire and need for meaningful administrative and clinical supervision in order to remain competent. Studies have found, however, that most school counselors are not receiving clinical supervision of any kind due to a lack of highly qualified school counselor supervisors (Kaffenberger, Murphy, & Bemak, 2006; Page, Pietrzak, & Sutton, 2001).

Limited qualified applicant pools have resulted in the promotion of practicing school counselors as a result of their performance as school counselors, or the promotion of individuals with higher education or supervisory experience in areas other than school counseling. Alas, proficiency as a school counselor or an administrator trained in other educational fields does not equal a proficient school counselor supervisor.

Although such practices may have been necessary, research has revealed that school counselor supervisors who lack specialized education in counselor supervision tend to shy away from the clinical aspects of enhancing counseling knowledge and skills, thereby providing insufficient clinical supervision (Herlihy et al., 2002). Insufficient clinical supervision, which includes the ethical and legal implications of counseling minors in the schools, leaves many school districts chronically vulnerable to litigation.

School counselors and others who aspire to provide administrative and clinical counselor supervision should seek to acquire advanced education and credentialing in preparation for such a role. It is not recommended that time spent in the role of school counselor be considered sufficient for promotion to counselor supervisor/director—it is not a rite of passage.

School counselors who have a passion for the profession, a desire to bring about change, and an aspiration to become highly competent, effective leaders will seek to enhance education and credentials above the minimal criteria for school counselor and contribute to the profession through research, service, presentation, and publication. These are the school counselors who have prepared for the clinical and administrative roles of counselor supervisor.

As noted earlier, school administrators can encourage advanced-level education and credentialing for school counselors by demonstrating this preference in promotion and selection decisions and offering stipends for advanced voluntary credentials—by both NBPTS and NBCC. In addition, pay supplements or higher salaries for school counselor directors and supervisors are a financial investment that will prove to have substantial returns for all stakeholders.

SUMMARY

Decades of political winds have shifted the educational climate, shaping our nation's schools. School counselors are continuously left out of educational reform agendas, viewed as noncontributors, and burdened with large student caseloads because we cannot provide evidence of how we are making a difference in the lives of students and how our programming has positively impacted academic achievement—the primary mission of schools.

Concern for the future of the profession and recognizing the need to align school counseling programs with academic achievement for optimal student services has prompted the need for an unparalleled change in school counseling. The new era requires continued shifts in both preparation and practice. It is an exciting and challenging time to be a part of the school counseling profession, with much work to be done and significant changes to be made—together.

CHAPTER 6

The Tool Box of the Century

The call for accountability in school counseling practices is not new, but dates back to the 1920s (Gysbers, 2004). The persevering demand has heightened efforts to prepare, encourage, and support school counselor efforts toward accountable practices. Throughout this text we have discussed data-driven practices, standards-based program planning, research-supported curriculum and counseling approaches, and program evaluation as a means of improving practices and demonstrating accountability. To further clarify the construct of accountability the following statement is offered: "To be accountable means being responsible for one's actions and contributions, especially in terms of objectives, procedures, and results" (Myrick, 2003, p. 175).

DAILY MATERIALS MOST FREQUENTLY
USED BY SCHOOL COUNSELORS

The materials used by school counselors as a part of daily practices and processes aid in demonstrating accountability, credibility, and cultural sensitivity. These processes further depict the school counselor's knowledge as it pertains to the ethical and legal practices of counseling minors in the school setting. This chapter identifies the daily materials most frequently used by school counselors. Since these materials, created using Microsoft Word, are not always provided or up-to-date in the preparation/practice setting, the accompanying CD includes the following materials for the purposes noted.

- Action Plan Template: School Counseling Operational Plan for Effectiveness (SCOPE)
- Case Notes (Essential Note-keeping Elements)
- Child Abuse Report (Suspected Child Abuse Reporting)
- Core School Counseling Curriculum Communication to Teachers (Beginning of Year)
- Informed Consent (Parental Consent for Small Groups/Individual Counseling Services)
- Informed Consent (Parental Consent for Sensitive Classroom Lessons/Assemblies)
- Opt Out of School Counseling Form
- Referral for School Counseling Services by Teacher/Administrator
- Referral for School Counseling Services by Parent
- Referral for School Counseling Services (Elementary Student Self-Referral)
- Referral for School Counseling Services (Secondary Student Self-Referral)
- Release of School Counseling Case Notes and Sharing of Information
- Results Report Template: School Counseling Operational Report of Effectiveness (SCORE)
- Suicide Ideation Report (Suspected Suicide Reporting)

Action Plans and Lesson Plans

ASCA has underscored the importance of actions plans and lesson plans in documenting program and lesson activities and the result of those activities on student development and academic achievement. Abraham Lincoln declared, "Give me six hours to chop down a tree and I will spend the first four sharpening the axe." Lincoln's statement clearly depicts the time-consuming and important nature of planning.

Action plans and lesson plans are important to share with stakeholders, namely school administrators, to gain the support of these important others. Studies indicate stakeholder support and partnerships enhance school climate and increase the likelihood of a student's success in school and in life (Bryan, 2005; Cooper, 2002). School counselors, who involve stakeholders in program planning and routinely provide stakeholders with information about school counseling activities aid in establishing positive alliances and gaining and maintaining program momentum.

The School Counseling Operational Plan for Effectiveness (SCOPE) is a Microsoft Office template intended to streamline action planning and lesson planning. SCOPE (see Figure 6.1) makes use of form check boxes and text boxes to walk the user through the process of accountable program planning. SCOPE meets the programming requirements and essential components of the ASCA (2012) recommended action plans, closing the achievement gap action plans, and lesson plans. It is recommended that SCOPE be used in partnership with SCORE, the School Counseling Operational Report of Effectiveness, which is the second part of the two-part data-reporting template discussed later in this chapter.

SCOPE
School Counseling Operational Plan for Effectiveness

School Counselor: Others:

Action Plan/Lesson Plan Date: Title:

☐ Small Group ☐ School Counseling Curriculum ☐ Individual Student Planning

Need/Purpose:

☐ Closing the Gap Strategy Data Used to Identify Gap Population:

Target Population: Students in Grade(s): Projected Number of Participants:
Other:

Goal:

Objective(s):

Core Subjects & Academic Standards Addressed:

☐ Mathematics
☐ Language Arts
☐ Science
☐ Social Studies
☐ Other

Domains & School Counseling Standards:

☐ Academic
☐ Personal/Social
☐ Career

Plan for Evaluation: ☐ Outcome ☐ Process ☐ Perception ☐ Proximal ☐ Distal
Data Sources:

Curriculum (Number of Sessions/Lessons: Timeline:):

Figure 6.1. Action Plan Template: School Counseling Operational Plan for Effectiveness (SCOPE)

Case Notes

Counseling session case notes need to be maintained in a confidential manner (e.g., locked in a filing cabinet). There are differences with regard to confidentiality/reporting requirements when referring to case notes that are sole possession notes and those that are formal case notes (Schellenberg, 2012). Formal case notes are objective in nature, while sole possession case notes are often more subjective.

Although, for now, school counseling case notes fall under the Family Educational Rights and Privacy Act (FERPA), school counselors are well-advised to consider the Health Insurance Portability and Accountability Act (HIPAA) when creating formal case notes. Reasons for this involve the advanced level of credentials many school counselors are beginning to earn that are supplemental to department of education school counselor licensure (Schellenberg, 2012). These credentials may, at some point in time, be viewed as equivalent to mental health care providers thus under the watchful eye of HIPAA. HIPAA requires specific objective formal case note information, which is noted below and included on the Case Notes form on the CD (see Figure 6.2):

- Dates of sessions
- Number of sessions
- Assessment data
- Presenting problem
- Treatment/counseling plan
- Information related to collaboration and consultation with others
- Session notes
- Associated documents (e.g., informed consent, drawings, letters, referrals

Child Abuse Report

There are multiple types of and many possible signs of child abuse and child neglect of which school counselors need to be aware (Schellenberg 2012). School counselors are mandated reporters of suspected child abuse and neglect. Information on violence prevention and child abuse and neglect along with mandated reporting requirements and

School Name (HERE)

School Counseling Case Notes

Counselor Name: _____   Date of session: _____

Student Name: _____   Session # _____ of _____

Presenting issue(s):

Assessment/Appraisal data:

Counseling Plan:

Collaboration/Consultation Information (Who, When, How, Why, What)

Session Notes (objective):

(Attach any related documents such as drawings, letters, referrals, informed consent)

Figure 6.2.   Case Notes (Essential Note-Keeping Elements)

Child Abuse and Neglect Training Modules are available at www. childwelfare.gov/preventing/developing/training.cfm.

School counselors are required to report suspected child abuse/ neglect within a specific time period, which is generally anywhere from twenty-four to seventy-two hours. School counselors need to know the law in their state as it pertains to reporting child abuse and neglect. The Child Abuse Report on the enclosed CD walks school counselors through reporting requirements (see Figure 6.3).

Core School Counseling Curriculum Communication to Teachers

School counselors generally supply teachers with a communication and core school counseling curriculum schedule at the beginning of each year. This communication may be emailed, placed in teacher

---

School Name HERE

Child Abuse/Neglect Reporting
(Know your state's reporting timeline, generally no more than 72 hours)

Student Name: _____   Grade: _____   Today's Date: _____

School Counselor Reporting: _____

Parent-Guardian: _____   Home Phone: _____ Work/Cell: _____

Who is suspected of the abuse/neglect? _____ Relationship to student: _____
       Address: _____   Phone: _____

Date suspected abuse occurred: _____   Time: _____   Place of suspected abuse: _____

Date suspected abuse reported to school counselor: _____ Time: _____

How was the suspected abuse disclosed: _____

Student's emotional state at the time of disclosure: _____

Names and ages of siblings: _____

Describe nature of suspected abuse (e.g., sexual, physical, emotional) or neglect (e.g., physical, educational), and identify specific body parts (scars, bruises, cuts, etc. do not have to be visible).
_____
_____
_____

Have the information above completed when contacting Child Protective Services/law enforcement.

Date of report by school counselor to CPS/law enforcement: _____   Time of report: _____

CPS/law enforcement Contact Name: _____

Information given to the CPS/law enforcement contact (based on information noted above):
_____
_____
_____

Time child or adolescent scheduled to leave school on date of report: _____

Let CPS/law enforcement know if child or adolescent needs to be seen immediately (e.g., child scared to go home, you are concerned for the child if they go home unaccompanied by CPS/law enforcement).

Actions taken by CPS/law enforcement:
_____
_____

Figure 6.3.   Child Abuse Report (Suspected Child Abuse Reporting)

boxes, and/or posted on electronic bulletin boards/intranet systems. The communication briefly introduces the school counselor's services and the process for services delivery. The document includes the schedule for delivery of core school counseling curriculum with an invitation to teachers to identify additional topics they would like the school counselor to address. The communication also offers teachers the opportunity to change the days/times of scheduled school counseling curriculum delivery for days/times more convenient to class schedule and planned activities. A general form is provided on the enclosed CD and may vary significantly, depending upon what the school counselor would like to relay to teachers at the start of each school year (see Figure 6.4).

Informed Consent

Two informed consent forms are included in the CD. One is for Parental Consent for Sensitive Classroom Lessons/Assemblies (see

---

Name of School HERE

Classroom Guidance Curriculum Communication to Teachers (Beginning of the Year)

Hello Teachers!

As you plan for a great year, I wanted to provide you with information about the services I offer to support you and your students. I offer small groups and individual counseling aimed at addressing the immediate needs of your students. The *Referral for School Counseling Services by Teacher/Administrator* is available in my office. Parents, too, may refer their child/adolescent for school counseling services. Please refer interested parents to me. I will be communicating my services to parents during our first PTA/PTSA meeting. Students may use the *Self-Referral* forms located in the box outside my office door, as needed. I will explain this procedure to students during the beginning of the year assembly.

[Secondary school counselors will also want to say, "I also offer individual student planning aimed at readying students for life after high school" and describe the process for reaching every student in your school.]

The classroom guidance schedule for each of your classes is listed below. Please let me know immediately if the date and time I have selected to deliver the guidance curriculum is not convenient and we will work together to select a day and time that is best for you. The topics are selected based on a review of school data and/or based on the delivery of a comprehensive school counseling program that attends to the developmental needs of students and addresses specific school counseling student standards and competencies. If you would like me to conduct additional guidance lessons for your class, please provide me with the topic you would like me to cover and we'll schedule a date and time for curriculum delivery.

Please do not hesitate to contact me if you have concerns about one or more of your students. I am here to support you in any way I can.

[Classroom Guidance Schedule Here]

Kindest regards,

Signature Here
Email Here

Figure 6.4. Core School Counseling Curriculum Communication to Teachers (Beginning of Year)

Figure 6.5). The other informed consent form is for Parental Consent for Small Group/Individual Counseling Services (see Figure 6.6).

Parental Consent for Sensitive Classroom Lessons/Assemblies should be obtained when the topic to be covered is sensitive or graphic in nature. For example, if a school counselor is implementing core school counseling curriculum titled "Internet Safety" and the content includes something akin to abduction, sexual assault, homicide, etc., then the school counselor will want to seek parental consent. Otherwise, school counselors do not generally seek parental consent for the delivery of core school counseling curriculum intended to be educational in nature and afforded to all students school-wide. When in doubt, err on the side of caution and provide the parent with an opportunity to opt the student out of such activities providing them with the topic, description, and the date and time of the activity.

School Name (HERE)

Sensitive Topic Classroom Guidance/Assembly Informed Consent

Dear Parent or Guardian,

This is to inform you that the school counselor(s) at your student's school is coordinating/conducting a classroom guidance lesson/assembly that involves information of a sensitive nature.

The topic to be covered is _____ and will be presented by
_____. The following are more details regarding the content of the program to be delivered:

(Insert curriculum to be covered in the activities/program HERE)

_____

Consent:

I, _____, have read and understand the contents of this informed consent.
    (please print name)

I give my child permission to participate in the proposed counseling activities/program.

Parent/Guardian Signature:_____ Date:_____

Figure 6.5. Informed Consent (Parental Consent for Sensitive Classroom Lessons/Assemblies)

School counselors are not legally obligated to obtain parental permission prior to group or individual counseling, unless there is a federal or state statute to the contrary (Remley & Herlihy, 2010; Stone, 2009). However, many school division policies require that school counselors obtain parental consent, particularly if counseling will extend beyond one or two sessions as a matter of best practices (Stone, 2009). For this reason, the second informed consent form in this text is for Parental Consent for Small Group/Individual Counseling Services.

School Name HERE
Parent/Guardian Consent for Individual and Group School Counseling Services

This is to inform you that your student, _____, has been referred to the school counselor by
_____ for concerns related to:

☐ Academic   ☐Behavior   ☐Interpersonal ☐ Personal   ☐ Career

School Counselor will conduct counseling services via:
☐Individual counseling ☐Individual student planning   ☐ Small group counseling

Topics to be covered during the counseling sessions may include one or more of the following:

☐Emotional Concerns   ☐Academic Performance   ☐ Career
☐Behavioral Concerns   ☐Interpersonal Relationships

Additional information: _____
_____

School counseling sessions are generally 20-30 minutes. Counseling sessions will take place in the school in an environment that supports the confidential nature of counselor-student relationship.
Confidentiality: Information revealed between the school counselor and student during the counseling session is confidential. It is the ethical responsibility of the counselor to safeguard students from unauthorized disclosures of information shared in the context of the counseling sessions. The school counselor seeks to establish alliances with parents and educators that are in the best interest of the student. Limitations to confidentiality include:

✓ When student poses danger to self, others, or the property of others.
✓ When counselor suspects abuse/neglect.
✓ Upon authorization of parent/student.
✓ Under court order.

In some circumstances school counselors may be required to breach confidentiality as a matter of school policy. These limitations will be discussed with students during initial counseling sessions. The importance of confidentiality is stressed during group sessions, but cannot be guaranteed between group members.

Consent:

I, _____, have read and understand the contents of this informed consent.
  (please print name)

I give my student permission to participate in the proposed school counseling services.

Parent/Guardian Signature:_____ Date:_____

Figure 6.6. Informed Consent (Parental Consent for Small Groups/Individual Counseling Services)

Opt Out of School Counseling

School counselors are strongly encouraged to ensure that every parent receives an Opt Out of School Counseling form (see Figure 6.7). Generally, this form is included in the student handbook. A parent who wishes to opt their child or adolescent out of individual counseling, individual student planning, and/or group counseling may complete and return the form to the school counselor. Even when a parent opts a student out of counseling services, the school counselor may see the student if that meeting is deemed essential to maintaining immediate order in the school.

Name of School HERE

Opt Out of School Counseling Services

Dear Parent or Guardian,

School counseling services are provided to your student as part of his or her educational services. If you **do not** wish to allow you student to participate in any of the services listed below please place a check mark by the service that you do not wish the school counselor to provide. Please keep in mind that even if you opt your child out of individual counseling services, a school counselor may have sessions with your child throughout the school year if doing so is warranted in order to maintain order in the school.

Individual student planning is not listed, since school counselors must meet with secondary level students for scheduling and academic/career planning. The school counselor's instructional curriculum delivered in the classroom is not listed since those services are a part of the school curriculum afforded to all students. If classroom instruction (or another program) by the school counselor is of a sensitive nature, you will be informed and allowed the opportunity to opt your student out of those specific programs. Thank you for the opportunity to work with your student!

Please do nothing if you want your child to participate in school counseling services as noted above.

Please place a check mark(s) by the school counseling service you wish to opt your student out of:

☐ Small Group Counseling   ☐ Individual Counseling

_____   _____
Name of Parent or Guardian (please print)   Name of Student (please print)

_____   _____
Parent/Guardian Signature   Date

Parent/Guardian Telephone Information:

Home: _____

Work: _____

Cell: _____

Figure 6.7.   Opt Out of School Counseling Form

Referral for School Counseling Services

Four of the Referral for School Counseling Services forms are included in the enclosed CD. One form is provided for each of the following populations: (1) teacher/administrator, (2) parent, (3) elementary self-referral, and (4) secondary self-referral. These forms are simplistic in nature to ease referral processes. The teacher/administrator form asks if the parent is aware of the issues and/or the referral to the school counselor. This is to promote parent-teacher relations. The parent should be made aware of concerns that the teacher and/or administrator are having with their child or adolescent prior to referral to the school counselor, unless the teacher or administrator suspects child abuse.

School Name HERE

Teacher and Administrator Referral for School Counseling Services

Referral Source: _____   Relationship to Student: _____

Student Name: _____   Grade: _____

Reason(s) for Referral: Academic _____ Behavior _____ Social _____ Personal _____

Please describe circumstances/concern: _____

_____

What strategies have been taken to date to mediate concern: _____

_____

_____

How might the concern noted be impacting the student academically, personally, and/or socially:

_____

Please explain any external factors that you feel the counselor needs to know: _____

_____

_____

Has the parent been informed of your concerns? _____ Yes _____ No

If not, please explain: _____

Has the parent been informed of this referral to school counseling services? ___ Yes _____ No

If not, please explain: _____

Figure 6.8.   Referral for School Counseling Services by Teacher/Administrator

---

School Name HERE

Parent Referral (consent included) for School Counseling Services

Student Name (please print full name): _____

Parent/Guardian Making Referral (please print): _____
      Relationship to Student: _____ (e.g., mother, father)

Reason(s) for Referral: Academic _____ Behavior _____ Social _____ Personal _____

Please describe circumstances/concern: _____
_____

What strategies have been taken to date to mediate concern: _____
_____

How might the concern noted be impacting the student academically, personally, and/or socially:
_____

Please explain any external factors that you feel the school counselor needs to know:
_____
_____

Has the teacher been informed of your concerns? _____ Yes _____ No
If not, please explain: _____

Has the teacher been informed of this referral to school counseling services? ___ Yes _____ No
If not, please explain: _____

Confidentiality: Information revealed between the school counselor and student during the counseling session is confidential. It is the ethical responsibility of the counselor to safeguard students from unauthorized disclosures of information shared in the context of the counseling sessions. The school counselor seeks to establish alliances with parents and educators that are in the best interest of the student. Limitations to confidentiality include:

   ✓ When student poses danger to self, others, or the property of others.
   ✓ When counselor suspects abuse/neglect.
   ✓ Upon authorization of parent/student.
   ✓ Under court order.

In some circumstances school counselors may be required to breach confidentiality as a matter of school policy. These limitations will be discussed with students during initial counseling sessions. The importance of confidentiality is stressed during group sessions, but cannot be guaranteed between group members.

Informed Consent:

I give my student permission to participate school counseling services.

Parent/Guardian Signature:_____   Date:_____

Figure 6.9.   Referral for School Counseling Services by Parent

Release of School Counseling Case Notes and Sharing of Information

Most schools have a release of records form, so school counselors should know the school's policy with regard to use of that form. In the absence of policy, a specific form, or if the school counselor is permitted to use their own form, the Release of School Counseling Case Notes and Sharing of Information is provided in the text CD (see Figure 6.12). School counselors must obtain written permission from the parent and assent from the student prior to sharing student informa-

School Name HERE

I Want to See the School Counselor

My Name is: _____

My Teacher is: _____

I am in grade: _____

Today's date is: _____

If you want to see the school counselor today draw a circle around the mouse!

Figure 6.10. Referral for School Counseling Services (Elementary Student Self-Referral)

tion. There are times when a school counselor is encouraged by the parent to share documents or communications with outside counselors (or others with a legitimate interest in the well-being of the student) to aid in helping the student. School counselors, who are comfortable sharing the information obtained in the counselor-student relationship with identified others should get parent permission in writing and ensure student assent.

School Name HERE

Please complete this form to see the school counselor:

Date:_____

Your Name: _____

My School Counselor's Name: _____

Do you need to see the school counselor today: Circle one: YES   NO

Please list your teachers and times in each class:

Teachers	Class Times

Figure 6.11. Referral for School Counseling Services (Secondary Student Self-Referral)

School Name HERE
Release of School Counseling Case Notes and Sharing of Information

Signing of this document authorizes the school counselor, _____, to release counseling case notes and to share counseling related information with _____ for the following student: _____.

The school counselor and parent/guardian have discussed the purpose of these communications with the above named student and the student is in agreement with the sharing of information between the school counseling and the above named professional.

This release form does not authorize release of academic records and other documents housed in the student's academic record. Parents seeking the release of information contained in the student's academic record should contact _____.

Consent:

I, _____, have read and understand the contents of this release form.
        (please print name)

I give permission to the school counselor named above, to release school counseling case notes and to freely communicate information shared by the student named above with the professional listed in this document.

Parent/Guardian Signature:_____ Date:_____

Figure 6.12.   Release of School Counseling Case Notes and Sharing of Information Form

Results Reports

Historically, service logs have been used to document time on task and illustrate the numerous and diverse duties and levels of responsibilities of the school counselor. Although services delivered have their value in identifying *what* it is that school counselors do from day-to-day, they are inadequate in an outcome-driven educational environment. As the axiom goes . . . *we are drowning in information, but starved for knowledge.* Documenting services delivered does not and should not replace program evaluation.

The knowledge we seek can be obtained by translating data into meaningful reports. Alas, this task can be time consuming and cumbersome while exacerbated by daunting workloads. Nonetheless, creating documents that demonstrate activity outcomes enhances accountability. The School Counseling Operational Report of Effectiveness (SCORE) is a Microsoft Office template intended to streamline the results reporting process and meet the essential component guidelines for results reporting and closing the achievement gap results reporting recommended by ASCA (2012). SCORE is the second part of a two-part data reporting template specifically designed for school counseling programs. SCORE used in partnership with SCOPE demonstrates essential components of a comprehensive school counseling program that aligns with academic achievement missions, documenting both action plans (or lesson plans) and results reports.

SCORE (see Figure 6.13) is designed to walk the user through the process of accountable program evaluation using form check boxes, text boxes, and drop-down menus. SCORE eases the process of data analysis, providing users with a preformulated Excel worksheet that contains protected formulas and accommodates up to five thousand data sets.

SCORE also allows for graphic illustrations as desired. Figure 6.14 illustrates what the user will see once the graph icon on the template is double-clicked. The user simply enters the pre- and post-program data and lets the spreadsheet do the rest.

The worksheet can be used to calculate means and percentages of difference for up to five thousand data sets. Pre- and post-program data are typed into columns A and B. The pre-program mean score appears in column C; the post-program mean score appears in column D. The percentage of difference from pre- to post-program measure appears in column E.

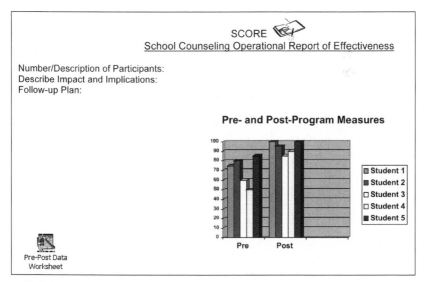

Figure 6.13. Results Report Template: School Counseling Operational Report of Effectiveness (SCORE)

Pre- and Post-Program Data Worksheet

Program Title:

Data Type:

Pre-Program Data	Post-Program Data	Pre-Program Data Mean	Post-Program Data Mean	Percentage of Change Pre- to Post-Program
		50	100	100%
50	100			

Figure 6.14. Pre- and Post-Program Date Worksheet

The SCORE worksheet can be used to analyze perception/outcome data for an entire school's population, individual students, a single class, multiple classes, grade levels, special populations, and specific question clusters for determining change/growth in targeted areas such as school counseling curriculum components, language arts components, and mathematics components. The worksheet can be copied for the inclusion of multiple worksheets in order to disaggregate data, or the worksheet can be deleted for exclusion from the report. The worksheet can also be saved (use the "save as" function) for storing data in a folder apart from the template.

SCORE allows the user to enhance results reporting with graphic representations. Remember—a picture is worth a thousand words! To complete the graph, double click on it and modify the content to reflect the data. Like the worksheet, the graph can be deleted, saved in a separate folder on your computer, and/or duplicated for multiple graphic representations.

Suicide Ideation Report

School counselors who suspect a child or adolescent may be suicidal should document these cases and make appropriate contacts. The Suicide Ideation Form in the text CD (see Figure 6.15), walks school counselors through the legally sound reporting processes. If you are required to use your school's form, please look for the following processes in the school's policy or on the form: (1) If a parent can be implicated as a reason for suicide ideation, then the parent should not contacted. Instead, contact Child Protective Services or other agencies identified in your school's policy and share information related to the student implicating the parent; (2) Outside counseling from a professional counselor pertaining to the student's emotional state should be obtained prior to returning to school. If numbers one and two above

---

School Name HERE

Suicide Prevention: Assessment and Reporting
(SCHOOL COUNSELING STUDENTS KNOW YOUR SCHOOL POLICIES AND KNOW THE LAWS IN YOUR STATE)
Students who express thoughts of suicide are considered to be at imminent risk of harm to self or others.

Student Name: _____   Grade: _____
Date of Incident: _____ Time of Incident: _____ Date of Report: _____ Time of Report: _____
School Counselor Reporting: _____
Parent-Guardian: _____ Home Phone: _____ Work/Cell: _____
Student expressed suicidal thoughts: ☐ verbally ☐ in writing ☐ in art ☐ Other
Describe: _____

Current Emotional State

☐ Guilt   ☐ Anxiety   ☐ Sadness   ☐ Flat Affect ☐ Helplessness☐ Other:_____
Describe: _____

Suicide Plan: ☐ Yes or ☐ No   Method:_____   Place:_____   Time: _____
Prior thoughts/threats of suicide? ☐ Yes or ☐ No
Describe: _____
Prior attempt? ☐ Yes or ☐ No   When? _____   Method: _____

Reporting Procedures:

1. Are student's thoughts of suicide related to alleged parental abuse or neglect, or are the parents implicated as a reason for suicide ideation? Yes or No *(if no skip # 2, if yes)*

2. When the parent/legal guardian is implicated as a reason for the student's thought of suicide, **DO NOT** contact the Parent. Contact the Child Protective Services in your city/county at (telephone number HERE).

   Social Services Contact Name: _____   Date: _____ Time: _____
   Describe: _____

3. Parent is contacted and asked if he or she is aware of the student's mental state: Yes   or   No

4. Ask the parent/legal guardian if he or she agrees to obtain professional counseling services for their child. Parents may wish to seek spiritual/religious counseling (see school division policy).

5. If the parent/legal guardian does not agree to obtain professional counseling services, a report is to be made to Child Protective Services, (telephone number HERE).

   Social Services Contact Name: _____   Date: _____ Time: _____
   Describe: _____

6. Keep student supervised until parent/legal guardian or a representative of Child Protective Services arrives. If a parent/legal guardian picks up the student, supply a list of counseling resources and obtain signature on this form.

I am aware that my child has expressed suicidal thoughts and I agree to obtain professional counseling services for my child to include a suicide assessment and safety plan.

_____   _____
Parent or Legal Guardian Signature   Date

Figure 6.15.   Suicide Ideation Report

are not a part of your school's policy or forms, please bring this to the attention of your school counseling division director and/or principal.

SUMMARY

Accountability in education and school counseling practices is a growing trend. Accountable practices necessitates that school counselors create action plans and results reports that identify data-driven, standards-based, and research-supported services, and specify program goals, procedures, and evaluative outcomes. Accountability is also establish through the daily use of reporting forms, letters, and other communications to demonstrate credible practices and processes that are culturally sensitive and ethically and legally sound.

Glossary

Adapted from The School Counselor's Study Guide for Credentialing Exams (Schellenberg, 2012).

academic development: one of three developmental domains within a comprehensive school counseling program that focuses on promoting skills, relating learning to life, and enhancing academic success and a positive attitude toward school and learning.

access data: data that assesses inequities in opportunities to participation in rigorous curriculum and school and community programs.

accommodation: adjustments made to instruction, homework, testing, and the physical environment in order to promote the success of students with special needs (e.g., special education, 504, and ESL students), as well as students with temporary conditions (e.g., illness, injury).

accountability: practices that are data-driven, standards-based, research-supported, evaluated for effectiveness and ongoing program improvement, and demonstrate "how" school counselors make a difference in the lives of students.

achievement data: in accordance with the ASCA National Model (2012), achievement data is data that assesses students' academic growth.

achievement gap: the disparity in educational performance that exists between specific populations of students—primarily low income and minority students—when compared to peers on a variety of educational measures, namely standardized tests.

action plan: written plans that describes specific programming and how programming will achieve stated objectives, including closing the achievement gap activities. SCOPE, the School Counseling Operational Plan for Effectiveness, is an example of ASCA-recommended action plans.

action research: research conducted for the purpose of enhancing the effectiveness of one's practices and/or measuring program outcomes.

active listening: a basic counseling skill and communication skill that attends to the student's verbal and nonverbal behaviors.

addiction: psychological and/or physiological dependence on a substance or activity.

advisory council: a committee of stakeholders established by the school counselor to direct and assist the school counseling program. ASCA recommends an advisory committee as part of the school counseling program management system to promote program success.

advocacy: a function of the school counselor that involves acting and speaking on behalf of others to support equity and access to programming, and to promote student, family, school, and community relations and development.

aggression: verbal, physical, and psychological behaviors intended to cause harm, threat, or pain.

Americans with Disabilities Act (ADA): national legislation that prohibits discrimination against persons with a disability in employment, public institutions, public transportation, and telecommunications. A qualified individual with a disability is entitled to reasonable accommodations.

anorexia: an eating disorder that is characterized primarily by a consistent and extreme restriction of food intake and a refusal to maintain a minimum normal body weight for age and height.

antisocial behavior: behavior, covert and overt, that disregards the rights and privacy of others, and the norms, laws, and standards of a society.

appraisal (*see also* assessment): approaches and/or measures (standardized and nonstandardized) used to gain a greater understanding of a student's functioning (e.g., intellectual, educational, mental, emotional, social, physical, occupational).

ASCA National Model: the only national model for the profession of school counseling designed to serve as a framework from which to implement a comprehensive, developmental and, primarily preventative, school counseling program.

ASCA National Standards: national standards (a foundational component of the ASCA National Model) that depict what students should know and be able to do as a result of a comprehensive school counseling program in three broad developmental areas: career, academic, and personal-social.

assessment (*see also* appraisal): approaches and/or measures (standardized and nonstandardized) used to gain a greater understanding of a student's functioning (e.g., intellectual, educational, mental, emotional, social, physical, occupational).

attainment data: data that assesses levels of completion (e.g., graduation rates, attendance rates, college acceptance rates, course completion rates).

behavior contract: a plan of action used for general education students to reduce or eliminate specific, observable, and measurable undesirable behaviors by applying specific interventions and rewards.

Behavior Intervention Plan (BIP): a plan of action, often part of an IEP for special education students, aimed at reducing or eliminating specific, observable, and measurable undesirable behaviors by applying individualized interventions and rewards.

behavioral data: in accordance with the ASCA National Model (2012), behavioral data is data that literature has found to be linked to academic achievement.

behavioral rehearsal: practicing new skills and behaviors for application outside of the counseling environment.

bibliotherapy: the use of books/literature in counseling toward established counseling goals.

bulimia: an eating disorder that is characterized primarily by reoccurring episodes of binging and purging (e.g., vomiting, laxatives) and a preoccupation with body weight.

bullying (*see also* cyberbullying): any verbal, nonverbal, or physical behavior intended to intimidate, threaten, harm, or cause physical, emotional, and/or psychological pain.

career awareness: the focus on career development at the elementary level that promotes students' knowledge of the world of work.

career counseling: counseling aimed at career development at a specific time and across the life span.

career development: one of three developmental domains of a comprehensive school counseling program that promotes students' identification of, and preparation for, desired post–high school occupations, education, and training, and relating school and the world of work.

career development inventories: instruments used to enhance a student's knowledge pertaining to occupational choices, self-knowledge (e.g., interests, values, skills), and education and training related to specific careers.

career exploration: the focus at the middle school level that enhances students' understanding of career opportunities and the link between school and work, developing an academic plan to meet postsecondary career choices.

career planning: the focus at the high school level that encourages students to continue to update and follow through on established career and academic plans for career readiness.

child abuse: harm toward a child caused by neglect or exploitation, and/or physical, emotional, psychological, or sexual mistreatment.

child neglect: failure to provide for the social, psychological, emotional, and biological needs of a child; failure to prevent suffering or to act on behalf of the child that places the child in imminent danger; behaviors that place the child in harm's way.

child study: a team approach to identifying and understanding the needs of a student who is not achieving academically in comparison to peers, or demonstrating physical, emotional, verbal, or psychological issues that are interfering with daily functioning.

closed group: groups that are no longer open to new membership once group facilitation begins.

collaboration: a function of the school counselor that involves working cooperatively with others toward a common goal.

Computer-Assisted Career Guidance Systems (CACGS): electronic systems designed to promote career readiness.

conflict resolution: the process by which students resolve conflict peacefully by engaging a variety of skills (e.g., problem solving, empathy, clarification, questioning, communication, negotiation).

consultation: a function of the school counselor that involves providing services in their area of expertise to other stakeholders (e.g., teachers, parents, school administrators).

convergent problem solving: higher order analytical thinking that draws information from resources for a single best solution.

core school counseling curriculum: planned and documented (e.g., action/lesson plans) curriculum that is comprehensive, developmental, preventative, and delivered to all students as a direct service via instruction and group activities.

crisis: traumatic or extremely stressful situations that require immediate action to secure the safety and well-being of students and others (e.g., suicide or homicide risk, post-student suicide, homicide, accidental death, terrorism, natural disaster, child abuse/neglect).

crosswalking: a strategy (and ASCA school counselor competency) that integrates ASCA student standards with other relevant standards such as core academic standards.

cyberbullying (*see also* bullying): any electronic (e.g., texting, Internet, email, chat rooms, social networks) behavior intended to intimidate, threaten, harm, or cause physical, emotional, and/or psychological pain.

data analysis: an examination of information that aids school counselors in identifying stakeholder needs, targeting programming, and determining program effectiveness and areas for improvement.

data-driven: programs, practices, and activities that are created based on an analysis of data.

diagnostic test: an assessment used to identify areas of academic competencies and areas of deficit.

direct student services: equitable, comprehensive, needs-driven school counseling services that support the personal/social, academic, and career development of all students via the school counseling core curriculum, individual student planning, and responsive services.

disability: a cognitive/psychological, behavioral, and/or physical impairment that limits one or more daily living functions.

disaggregated data: the separation and analysis of data by specific variables to identify student populations who are performing at lower levels and to ensure equity and access.

divergent problem solving: higher order holistic thinking that draws information from fresh, more creative perspectives and across disciplines for multiple possible solutions.

educational diagnostician: an individual employed by school divisions to assess levels of student academic functioning and to suggest interventions to meet individual student needs; often a member of child study teams.

emancipated minor: a minor who has been granted by the courts the decision-making power of an adult with regard to their own affairs. Emancipated minors do not need parental consent to engage in counseling services.

encapsulation: ignorance of one's cultural background and how culture impacts one's total being.

English as a Second Language (ESL): student's whose primary or native language is not English.

equity: eliminating barriers to rigorous curriculum and school and community programs and promoting systemic policies, practices, and programs that establish and nurture culturally sensitive and culturally responsive environments.

extrinsic motivation: motivation that is achieved with external rewards (e.g., stickers, certification, treats, praise).

Family Educational Rights and Privacy Act (FERPA): legislation enacted to protect the privacy of students' academic records, and to allow parents and students to inspect academic records and petition for the removal of information perceived as inaccurate. FERPA is also known as the Buckley Amendment.

504 Plan: a written document that identifies special accommodations afforded to students with qualifying conditions pursuant to Section 504 of the Rehabilitation Act of 1973.

Free and Appropriate Public Education (FAPE): legislation that ensures individualized curriculum that meets unique student needs and prepares students for post–high school education, careers, and independent living.

General Equivalency Diploma (GED): an alternative to a high school diploma and completion of high school, the GED established mastery of high school core course content and may be obtained during the high school years through alternative educational programs or post–high school for those adults who "dropped out" of high school.

guidance counselor: an outdated title for the counselor in the pre-K–12 school setting, depicting only one component of the many functions of the contemporary school counselor that is associated primarily with more directive approaches and education and career planning.

high-stakes testing: standardized testing used to determine pass or failure of select core courses, graduation from high school, and drives the type of diploma received.

In Loco Parentis: a common-law doctrine that allows educators to act as parents, protecting students and their rights while under their care at school.

inclusion classroom: a general education classroom that provides additional supports and accommodations for special education student participation.

indirect student services: equitable, comprehensive school counseling services that support the personal/social, academic, and career development of all students using referrals for additional assistance/resources, collaboration with parents, educators, and community agencies, and by consultation with others to share and receive information useful in promoting student academic achievement, and development and well-being.

individual-focused: school counseling practices that are more focused on intervention for a select individual versus prevention and intervention services for all students.

individual student planning: a systemic direct student service that aids students in developing academic, personal, and career strategies for future plans and goal attainment via appraisal and advisement.

Individualized Education Program (IEP): a written document that identifies specific and individualized strategies for the personal-social, academic, and career success of students with a qualifying disability under IDEA as part of special education services.

Individuals with Disabilities Education Act (IDEA): national legislation that ensures that the educational needs of students with disabilities are met.

intelligence quotient (IQ): a score from standardized intelligence tests that represents one's level of intelligence.

intelligence test: standardized tests intended to assess an individual's cognitive abilities and yield an intelligence quotient score.

intervention: activities and strategies applied with the purpose of reducing or eliminating specific thoughts, actions, or situations.

intrinsic motivation: motivation that is achieved with internal rewards (e.g., specific positive feedback, earned recognition through accomplishment).

leadership: the ability to inspire, influence, and persuade others to follow or act.

learning profile: a comprehensive conceptualization that considers an individual's learning styles, predisposition toward specific intelligences (*see* **multiple intelligences**), as well as cultural and gender differences.

least restrictive environment: special education students are to receive educational services that promote success in the least restrictive manner, while receiving accommodations and supports as outlined in the student's IEP; least restrictive environments in the public school setting are the general education classrooms (*see also* **inclusion classroom**).

Limited English Proficient (LEP): individuals whose first language is not English, and are therefore restricted in their English-speaking ability.

medical plan: used in schools for students with medical conditions that might warrant special accommodations for a specified amount of time.

modeling: observing and imitating others.

motivation: a force, energy, desire, or state of being that directs thoughts and behavior.

multicultural counseling: counseling that is sensitive to the needs of all people and their unique worldviews grounded in gender, race, ethnicity, culture, social status, economic status, sexual orientation, and religion.

multiple intelligences: eight independent cognitive and affective intelligences working interactively for a holistic understanding of human intelligence.

needs assessment: formal and information measures that result in the identification of stakeholder needs.

negative reinforcement: removal of a stimulus in an effort to increase a desired behavior/response.

New Vision School Counseling: the movement to transform school counseling into an academic- and systems-focused paradigm.

No Child Left Behind (NCLB): legislation that supports standards-based education, the measurement of goals to enhance academic outcomes, and close achievement gaps between specific class and racial groups of students.

nontraditional occupation: occupations in which few individuals of a specific gender generally work. For example, occupations historically dominated by females would be nontraditional occupations for males (e.g., nurse), and occupations historically dominated by males would be nontraditional for females (e.g., mechanic).

Occupational Information Network (O*Net): national database for career information, exploration, assessment, and career decision-making.

Occupational Outlook Handbook **(OOH):** nationally recognized source for career information and career decision-making.

open group: groups that allow new membership once group facilitation begins.

outcome evaluation/data: program evaluation/data that assesses the effectiveness of a program/activity in meeting established goals and objectives.

paraphrasing: a basic counseling technique that involves the school counselor restating what a student has shared to communicate understanding.

peer helping: programs that involve students helping students (e.g., peer tutoring, peer mentoring, peer mediation).

peer mediation: a process by which students help students to resolve conflict peacefully by engaging a variety of skills (e.g., problem-solving, empathy, clarification, questioning, communication, negotiation). Peer mediation involves more than two individuals.

perception evaluation/data: program evaluation/data that assesses participants' opinions about their own thoughts, beliefs, feelings, and abilities.

personal-social development: one of three developmental domains within a comprehensive school counseling program that promotes total student well-being through the application of counseling theory and techniques, and teaches skills for living (e.g., safety, problem-solving, decision making, conflict resolution, communication).

play therapy: the use of directive and nondirective play facilitated by the school counselor as a therapeutic medium for emotional expression and communication.

positive reinforcement: application of a stimulus in an effort to increase a desired behavior/response.

prevention: activities and strategies applied with the purpose of averting specific thoughts, actions, or situations.

primary prevention: programming that focuses on prevention and wellness for a large population (e.g., entire student body), who may or may not be potentially at risk for a specific targeted behavior/problem.

process evaluation/data: program evaluation/data that describes the event/program and the number of participants impacted by the activity.

professional associations: school counseling related associations that support the profession with resources, professional development opportunities, unification, and advocacy.

professional school counselor: the contemporary title for the counselor in the pre-K–12 school setting, depicting a comprehensive counseling specialty that shares the dual roles of educator and counselor and practices using a comprehensive developmental model.

program evaluation: an ongoing component of accountable school counseling practices that results in data that demonstrates program outcomes and answers the question—"How do school counselors make a difference in the lives of students?"—and provides information for program improvement.

reciprocal determinism: a term coined by Albert Bandura to describe how behavior is determined by the shared relationship (one acting upon the other) between a person and the environment.

reinforcement/reinforcer (*see also* negative reinforcement; positive reinforcement): a concept used in operant conditioning to refer to a stimulus, positive or negative, to increase the likelihood of desired behaviors or reduce/eliminate undesired behaviors.

research-based: school counseling practices and programming that supported by research.

resilience: the capacity of an individual to cope with stress and harsh conditions.

response to intervention: an intervention process used to help struggling students to improve behavior and achieve academically.

responsive services: direct student services that meet the immediate needs and concerns of students, including crisis response via short-term, goal-focused individual and small group counseling.

results report: written reports that describes the outcomes of specific programming as outlined in action plans, including closing the achievement gap activities. SCORE, the School Counseling Operational Report of Effectiveness is an example of an ASCA-recommended results report.

risk factors: any physical, personal, social, familial, environmental, economical condition that places student's at a disadvantage and serves as an obstacle to well-being, academic achievement, and healthy student development.

school nurse: an individual employed by school divisions to attend to student injury, coordinate medical care with physicians, psychologists, and parents, and to administer medications during the school day; often a member of child study teams.

school psychologist: an individual employed by school divisions to assess levels of student psychological functioning and to suggest interventions to meet individual student needs; often a member of child study teams.

school social worker: an individual employed by school divisions to assess levels of student social and family functioning and to suggest interventions to meet individual student needs; often a member of child study teams.

School-to-Work Opportunities Act: legislation that seeks to ensure that students will be well-prepared to succeed in our multifaceted and technologically advanced workforce.

secondary prevention: programming aimed at mediating a specific behavior or problem that has been identified as a potential threat among a particular population or subgroup of students.

social justice: a moral and ethical movement toward creating a socially just world through an equitable distribution of resources to ensure personal, social, career, and academic development and well-being.

social responsibility: a moral and ethical ideology that is grounded in the principles of equality, unity, respect for human rights, and acting on behalf of the good of a society.

Socratic dialogue: inquiry or questioning aimed at exploring an individual's thoughts and/or knowledge pertaining to a specific topic.

special needs students: students who are limited English proficient, or have a 504 plan or IEP.

standards: statements that delineate what students should know and be able to do.

strengths-based counseling: a counseling approach that emphasizes the value of protective factors in combating risk factors and enhancing resilience.

Section 504: A part of the Americans with Disabilities Act (ADA), also known as the Rehabilitation Act of 1973, that protect individuals with disabilities from discrimination and allows for equal access to services and the provision of reasonable accommodations related to the disability.

stakeholders: any individual/organization that impacts or is impacted by the school.

Student Council Association: a program sponsored by educators to develop students' leadership and interpersonal skills while promoting school and community spirit and involvement.

substance abuse: repeated use of a chemical substance that may or may not include dependence.

substance use: repeated use of a chemical substance without dependence.

suicide assessment: screening an individual to determine their risk for suicide.

suicide ideation: thinking about taking one's own life.

summarizing: a basic counseling technique whereby the school counselor condenses into a few brief statements that which the student has conveyed over a period of time during the counseling session.

systems-focused: school counseling practices that are more focused on prevention and intervention services for all students versus a select few.

teaming: joining together with other stakeholders to accomplish a common goal.

tertiary prevention: programming that targets a specific population who are already engaging in the at-risk behavior or experiencing a specific problem in order to reduce or eliminate the problem or behavior and improve quality of life.

Transforming School Counseling Initiative (TSCI): the movement to change the paradigm of school counseling to one that is academic- and systems-focused.

universal academic achievement: academic achievement for all students.

wellness: a sense of personal, social, emotional, physical, and spiritual well-being.

worldview: how an individual conceptualizes and interprets the world, views their relationship with the world, and interacts with a world that is grounded in presupposition, beliefs, and values.

zeitgeist: the thought or spirit of the time in a specified time period or generation.

References

Agnew, T., Vaught, C., Getz, H., & Fortune, J. (2000). Peer group clinical supervision program fosters confidence and professionalism. *Professional School Counseling, 4*, 6–12.

American Counseling Association (ACA). (1987). *School counseling: A profession at risk.* Alexandria, VA: Author.

American Counseling Association (ACA). (2005). *Code of ethics and standards of practice.* Alexandria, VA: Author.

American Evaluation Association. (1994). Guiding principles for evaluators. *New Directions for Program Evaluation, 66*, 19–26.

American School Counselor Association. (2008). *ASCA position statements.* Retrieved from http://www.schoolcounselor.org.

American School Counselor Association (ASCA). (2010). *Ethical standards for school counselors.* Alexandria, VA: Author.

American School Counselor Association. (2012). *ASCA national model: A framework for school counseling programs* (3rd ed.). Alexandria, VA: Author.

Anderson, L. W., & Krathwohl, D. R. (Eds.). (2001). *A taxonomy for learning, teaching, and assessing: A revision of Bloom's Taxonomy of educational objectives.* New York: Longman.

Arbuckle, D. S. (1961). The conflicting functions of the school counselor. *Counselor Education and Supervision, 1*, 54–59.

Association for Assessment in Counseling and Education. (1998). *Competencies in assessment and evaluation for school counselors.* Retrieved from http://aac.ncat.edu/resources.html.

Auger, R. W. (2004). Responding to terror: The impact of September 11 on K–12 schools and schools' responses. *Professional School Counseling, 7*, 222–31.

Beale, A. V. (1995). Selecting school counselors: The principal's perspective. *The School Counselor*, *42*, 211–17.

Bloom, B. S. (1953). Thought processes in lectures and discussions. *Journal of General Education*, *7*, 160–69.

Bryan, J. (2005). Fostering educational resilience and achievement in urban schools through school-family-community partnerships. *Professional School Counseling*, *8*, 219–28.

Burnham, J. J., & Jackson, C. M. (2000). School counselor roles: Discrepancies between actual practice and existing models. *Professional School Counseling*, *4*, 41–49.

Campbell, C. A., & Dahir, C. A. (1997). *Sharing the vision: The national standards for school counseling programs.* Alexandria, VA: American School Counselor Association Press.

Center for School Counseling Outcome Research and Evaluation (2000). Retrieved from www.umass.edu/schoolcounseling.

Cooper, B. S. (2002). *Promises and perils facing today's superintendents.* New York: Rowman & Littlefield.

Council for Accreditation of Counseling and Related Educational Programs (CACREP). (2009). *CACREP accreditation standards and procedures manual* (5th ed.). Alexandria, VA: Author.

Crutchfield, L. B., & Borders, L. D. (1997). Impact of two clinical peer supervision models on practicing school counselors. *Journal of Counseling and Development*, *75*, 219–30.

Dilley, J., Foster, W., & Bowers, I. (1973). Effectiveness ratings of counselors without teaching experience. *Counselor Education and Supervision*, *13*, 24–29.

The Education Trust. (1997, February). *The national guidance and counseling reform program.* Washington, DC: Author.

Eschenauer, R., & Hayes, C. (2005). The transformative individual school counseling model: An accountability model for urban school counselors. *Professional School Counseling*, *8*, 244–49.

Gardner, H. (1983). *Frames of mind: The theory of multiple intelligences.* New York: Basic Books.

Gardner, H., & Moran, S. (2006). The science of multiple intelligences theory: A response to Lynn Waterhouse. *Educational Psychologist*, *41*(4), 227–32.

Gladding, S. T. (2001). *The counseling dictionary.* Upper Saddle River, NJ: Merrill-Prentice Hall.

Goddard, R. D., Hoy, W. K., & Woolfolk, H. A. (2000). Collective teacher efficacy: Its meaning, measure, and impact on student achievement. *American Educational Research Journal*, *37*, 479–507.

Guerra, P. (1998, April). Reaction to DeWitt Wallace grant overwhelming: Readers sound off on February *Counseling Today* article. *Counseling Today*, 13–20.

Gysbers, N. C. (2004). Comprehensive guidance programs: The evolution and accountability. *Professional School Counseling, 8*, 1–14.

Hardesty, P. H., & Dillard, J. M. (1994). Analysis of activities of school counselors. *Psychological Reports, 74*, 447–50.

Houser, R. (1998). *Counseling and educational research.* Thousand Oaks, CA: Sage.

Ingersoll, R. E., & Bauer, A. (2004). An integral approach to spiritual wellness in school counseling. *Professional School Counseling, 7*, 301–8.

Kaffenberger, C. J., Murphy, S., & Bemak, F. (2006). School counseling leadership team: A statewide collaborative model to transform school counseling. *Professional School Counseling, 9*, 288–95.

Kimbel, T., & Schellenberg, R. (n.d.). *Meeting the holistic needs of students: A proposal for spiritual and religious competencies for school counselors.* Unpublished manuscript.

Mark, T. (2011). Where have the parents gone? *Principal, 91*, 46-46.

Marzano, R. J. (2004). *Building background knowledge for academic achievement: Research on what works in schools.* Alexandria, VA: Association for Supervision and Curriculum Development.

Myrick, R. D. (2003). Accountability: Counselors count. *Professional School Counseling, 6*, 174–89.

National Council of Teachers of English (NCTE). (1996). Standards for the English language arts. Newark, DE: International Reading Association.

National Council of Teachers of Mathematics (NCTM). (2000). Principles and standards for school mathematics. Reston, VA: Author.

No Child Left Behind Act of 2001, Pub. L. No. 107–110.

Olson, M. J., & Allen, D. N. (1993). Principals' perceptions of the effectiveness of school counselors with and without teaching experience. *Counselor Education and Supervision, 33*, 10–21.

Page, B. J., Pietrzak, D. R., & Sutton, J. M. (2001). National survey of school counselor supervision. *Counselor Education and Supervision, 41*, 142–51.

Paisley, P. O., & Hayes, R. L. (2002). Transformations in school counselor preparation and practice. *Counseling and Humand Development*, 35, 1–10.

Paisley, P. O., & Hayes, R. L. (2003). School counseling in the academic domain: Transformations in preparation and practice. *Professional School Counseling, 6*, 198–205.

Peterson, J. S., Goodman, R., Keller, T., & McCauley, A. (2004). Teachers and non-teachers as school counselors: Reflections on the internship experience. *Professional School Counseling, 7*, 246–56.

Posavac, E. J., & Carey, R. G. (2003). *Program evaluation: Methods and case studies* (6th ed.). Upper Saddle River, NJ: Prentice Hall.

Poynton, T. A., & Carey, J. C. (2006). An integrative model of data-based decision making for school counseling. *Professional School Counseling, 10*, 121–31.

Rayburn, C. (2004). Assessing students for morality education: A new role for school counselors, *Professional School Counseling, 7*, 356–62.

Remley, T., & Herlihy, B. (2010). *Ethical, legal, and professional issues in counseling* (3rd ed.). Upper Saddle River, NJ: Pearson.

Ritchie, M., & Bobby, C. (2011, August 12). *Working together hand-in-hand: The common goals of CACREP and state counselor licensure boards.* A presentation at NBCC's 2011 State Licensure Board Meeting, Greensboro, NC.

Schellenberg, R. (2007). Standards blending: Aligning school counseling programs with school academic achievement missions. *Virginia Counselors Journal, 29*, 13–20.

Schellenberg, R. (2008). *The new school counselor: Strategies for universal academic achievement.* Lanham, MD: Rowman & Littlefield Education.

Schellenberg, R. (2012). *The school counselor's study guide for credentialing exams.* New York: Taylor & Francis/Routledge Publishing.

Schellenberg, R., & Grothaus, T. (2009). Promoting cultural responsiveness and closing the achievement gap with standards blending. *Professional School Counseling, 12*, 440–49.

Schellenberg, R., & Grothaus, T. (2011). Using culturally competent responsive services to improve student achievement and behavior. *Professional School Counseling, 14*, 222–230.

Schellenberg, R., Parks-Savage, A., & Rehfuss, M. (2007). Reducing levels of elementary school violence with peer mediation. *Professional School Counseling, 10*, 475–81.

Schellenberg, R., Pritchard, T., & Szapkiw, A. (n.d.). *Meeting the needs of the many and the few: A culturally competent guidance curriculum to enhance student achievement and career readiness.* Unpublished manuscript.

Search Institute (2007). Developmental assets list. Retrieved from www.search-institute.org/developmental-assets/lists.

Seligman, L. (2004). Diagnosis and treatment planning in counseling. *Professional School Counseling, 2*, 244–47.

Shoffner, M. F., & Williamson, R. D. (2000). Engaging preservice school counselors and principals in dialogue and collaboration. *Counselor Education and Supervision, 40*, 128–41.

Sink, C. (2005). *Contemporary school counseling: Theory, research, and practice*. Boston: Houghton Mifflin.

Sink, C. (2011). School-wide responsive services and the value of collaboration. *Professional School Counseling, 14*, ii–iv.

Stone, C. (2009). *School counseling principles, ethics, and law*. Alexandria, VA: American School Counseling Association.

Stone, S. J., & Chakraborty, B. (2011). Parents as partners: Tips for involving parents in your classroom. *Childhood Education, 87*, 344–44.

Sutton, C. M. (2006). The leader's role in reaching universal success for all. *School Administrator, 63*, 47.

U.S. Department of Education. (1996). *Companion document: Crosscutting guidance for the Elementary and Secondary Education Act*. Washington, DC: Author.

U.S. Department of Education. (2004). *Helping practitioners meet the goals of No Child Left Behind*. Washington, DC: Author.

U.S. House of Representatives 109th Congress. (2006). House Report 109–143, Departments of Labor, Health and Human Services, and Education, and Related Agencies Appropriation Bill, 2006. Washington, DC: Library of Congress.

Van Horn, S. M., & Myrick, R. D. (2001). Computer technology and the 21st century school counselor. *Professional School Counseling, 5*, 124–30.

Vansteenkiste, M., Lens, W., & Deci, E. L. (2006). Intrinsic versus extrinsic goal contents in self-determination theory: Another look at the quality of academic motivation. *Educational Psychologist, 41*, 19–29.

White, F. A. (2007). The professional school counselor's challenge: Accountability. *Journal of Professional Counseling, Practice, Theory, and Research, 35*(2), 62–70.

Wolf, J. T. (2004). Teach, but don't preach: Practical guidelines for addressing spiritual concerns of students. *Professional School Counseling, 7*, 363–66.

Index

ACA. *See* American Counseling Association

academic achievement of students, 1–5, 11–14, 46–53, 67–70, 77

academic development, 22, 68

academic-focused programming, 29, 63; ASCA and TSCI on achievement gap, 3, 11; school administrator and school counselor leadership alliance, 2, 12–13

academic mission of schools, 3, 13–14, 22

academic planning, for invisible student, 33

accountability, 48, 56, 63, 81, 98

ACES. *See* Association for Counselor Education and Supervision

achievement gap, 4, 6, 46, 77; action plan, 83; ASCA and TSCI academic-focused programming on, 3, 11; standards blending and, 51–53

action plan, 69, 82–83, *83*

action research, program evaluation as, 55, 59

advanced credentialing funding, 10

advanced voluntary credentials, 79, 80

advisory council, 15

advocacy, of New Vision School Counselor, 71–72

alignment approaches, in standards blending, 46–47

American Counseling Association (ACA): *Code of Ethics and Standards of Practice*, 61; *School Counseling: A Profession at Risk* report, 1–3

American School Counselor Association (ASCA): on action plans and lesson plans, 82; advisory council recommendation, 15; *Ethical Standards for School Counselors*, 34–35, 55, 61; goals provided by, 21; peer programming ethical guidelines, 42; SCALE of, 10–11; on school counselor role and functions, 27; on school counselor supervisor, 78. *See also* National Model; National Standards

analysis of variance (ANOVA), 59
applied research. *See* action research
appraisal, *32*, *38*, 50
ASCA. *See* American School
   Counselor Association
assessment, 52, 62, 65. *See also*
   needs assessment
Association for Counselor Education
   and Supervision (ACES), 6–7

behavioral data, 16, 31
best practices application, 22
bibliotherapy, 40
Bloom, Benjamin S., 24, *24*
Bloom's Taxonomy learning
   levels, 24, *24*; preservice school
   counselors and, 64; standards
   blending and, 48–49
bodily kinesthetic intelligence, 23,
   23

CACREP. *See* Council for
   Accreditation of Counseling and
   Related Educational Programs
career development, 6, 46, 48–49,
   71
career exploration, 40, 50–51
career planning, for invisible
   student, 33
Carey, J. C., 18
Carey, R. G., 61
case notes, 84, *85*
Center for School Counseling
   Outcome Research and
   Evaluation (CSCORE), 5–6
change agent: New Vision School
   Counseling as, 4, 68; proactive,
   42–44
child abuse report, 84–86, *86*
Child Protective Services, 97

children, needs assessment for,
   19–20
child study team, 30
classroom, standards blending
   beyond, 69
clinical competence, 9, 28, 64
*Code of Ethics and Standards of
   Practice*, ACA, 61
collaboration, 41; for mental health
   services, 4, 30; with stakeholders,
   15; standards blending for, 72; for
   student safety, 64
collaborative research, 57, 65, 67
Committee on Appropriations, on
   NBPT's credentialing, 10
Competencies for Addressing
   Spiritual and Religious Issues in
   Counseling, 36
Competencies in Assessment
   and Evaluation for School
   Counselors, 61
confidentiality, of case notes, 84
conflict resolution, 20, 40, 43
consultation, 15, 41
core school counseling curriculum,
   40, 65, 86–87
Council for Accreditation of
   Counseling and Related
   Educational Programs
   (CACREP): on clinical
   competence of school counselor,
   28; counselor education core
   areas, 6; NCC credential on
   standards of, 8; preservice school
   counselors and, 65–66; school
   counseling specialty standards,
   7; on school counselor roles and
   functions, 27; standards, 73;
   standards blending and, 65
counseling programs accreditation, 6

credentials: advanced, NBCC and NBPTS on, 8; advanced voluntary, 79, 80; progressive, 74

crosswalking, 48–49; approach, standards blending and, 47, 65; curriculum, 64–65

CSCORE. *See* Center for School Counseling Outcome Research and Evaluation

curriculum: core school counseling, 40, 65, 86–87; crosswalking, 64–65; development, on spiritual/religious development, 35; small-group, 51; standards blending and, 49

curriculum development, research-supported, 21–25; Bloom's Taxonomy learning levels, 24, *24*; Marzano's instructional strategies, 24, *25*; multiple intelligence theory, *23*, 23–24; on self-esteem, 22–23; theory of learning style, 25

data analysis, for program redesign, 15

data-driven program, 55; planning, 16–20; RTI and PBSI as, 31

departmental Web sites, 70

developmental assets, Search Institute on, 33

direct student services, 38–39, 49

distal evaluation, 58

educational practices, accountability in, 48

educator, school counselor role of, 9–10, 27, 44–46

Elementary and Secondary Education Act (ESEA), 36

ethical and legal considerations of research, 61

Ethical Standards for School Counselors, ASCA: on research, 55, 61; on student values, beliefs, 34–35

evidence-based practices, 48

Family Educational Rights and Privacy Act (FERPA), 84

focus groups, 18

formal case notes, 84

formative evaluations. *See* process evaluation/data

Gardner, Howard, multiple intelligences of, *23*, 23–24

goals, from needs assessment, 20–21

Guiding Principles for Evaluators, 61

Health Insurance Portability and Accountability Act (HIPAA), 84

holistic development of students, 2, 66, 77

indirect student services, 14, 39–40

individual student planning, 33, 40

informed consent: Parental Consent for Sensitive Classroom Lessons/Assemblies, 87–88, *88*; Parental Consent for Small Group/Individual Counseling Services, 88, 89, *89*

instructional competence, 9–10

instructional strategies, of Marzano, 24, *25*

interpersonal intelligence, 23, *23*

intervention, 7, 22, 29–30, 56, 58, 71

intrapersonal intelligence, 23, *23*

invisible student. *See* students,
  invisible

leadership alliances, with school
  administrators, 2, 12–13
learning profile, 48
learning style, theory of, 25
lesson plans, 82–83, *83*
Licensed Professional Counselor
  (LPC), for supervisor credentials,
  78–79
linguistic intelligence, 23, *23*
logical-mathematical intelligence,
  23, *23*
LPC. *See* Licensed Professional
  Counselor

MANOVA. *See* multivariate analysis
  of variance
Marzano, Robert, instructional
  strategies of, 24, *25*
measurable objectives. *See*
  objectives, measurable
mental health-focused paradigm,
  3–4, 11, 29, 76
mental health services, collaboration
  and referral for, 4, 30
Metropolitan Life Insurance
  Company (MetLife), TSCI and,
  5
motivation, 11, 49, 77
multicultural counseling, 35
multiple intelligences, of Gardner,
  23, 23–24, 48
multivariate analysis of variance
  (MANOVA), 59
musical intelligence, 23, *23*

National Board for Certified
  Counselors (NBCC), 7–10;

advanced voluntary credentials
  of, 80; credentialing, 10, 27
National Board for Professional
  Teaching Standards (NBPTS),
  44; advanced voluntary
  credentials of, 80; on counselor
  as educator, 9–10; credentialing,
  10, 27; NBCC and, on advanced
  credentialing, 8
National Center for Transforming
  School Counseling (NCTSC), 5
National Certified Counselor (NCC)
  credential: CACREP and NBCC
  standards for, 8; for supervisor,
  78–79
National Certified School Counselor
  (NCSC), for supervisor
  credentials, 78–79
National Model, ASCA (2012),
  1, 10, 11, 73; advisory council
  guidelines, 15; preservice school
  counselors and, 65; on spiritual/
  religious development, 36, 40
National School Counselor Training
  Initiative (NSCTI), 5
National Standards, ASCA, 3, 10, 47
naturalistic intelligence, 23, *23*
NBCC. *See* National Board for
  Certified Counselors
NBPTS. *See* National Board for
  Professional Teaching Standards
NCC. *See* National Certified
  Counselor
NCLB. *See* No Child Left Behind
NCSC. *See* National Certified
  School Counselor
NCTSC. *See* National Center for
  Transforming School Counseling
needs assessment, 15; for children,
  19–20; focus groups, 18; goals

from, 20–21; initial questions in, 19; on participant perceptions, 18–19; for special needs students, 19–20; stakeholder, 18, 25

New Vision School Counseling, 5, 63–80; as change agents, 4, 68; counselor educators, 63–64; pedagogy, 64–68; school administrator, 76–77; school counselor selection, by supervisor, 73–74; supervisor, 72–76; support of, 77–80

New Vision School Counselor: advocacy of, 71–72; professional identity of, 71–72; programming, 68–70; technology transitioning of, 70–71

No Child Left Behind (NCLB), 47

noncounseling duties, of school counselors, 77

nonexperimental research designs, 59

NSCTI. *See* National School Counselor Training Initiative

objectives, measurable, *21*

opt out of school counseling, 90, *90*

outcome evaluation data, 16, 57–58

paired sample t-tests, 59

parent: referral for school counseling services by, 91, *92*; teaming with, 69; volunteers, 43

Parental Consent for Sensitive Classroom Lessons/Assemblies informed consent, 87, *88*

Parental Consent for Small Group/ Individual Counseling Services informed consent, 88, 89, *89*

Parent-Teacher-Student Resource Center (PTSRC), 43

participant perceptions, needs assessment on, 18–19

PBSI. *See* Positive Behavioral Support

pedagogy, of New Vision School Counselor, 64–68

peer mediation, 42, *60*

peer programming, ASCA ethical guidelines for, 42

perception evaluation/data, 16, 57–58

personal-social development, 12, 47

Posavac, E. J., 61

Position Statements, ASCA, 35

Positive Behavioral Support (PBSI), 30–31

practice, bridging of theory and, 65–67

prayer in public schools, ESEA protection of, 36

preservice school counselors, 45, 63; Bloom's Taxonomy and, 64; CACREP and, 65–66; collaborative research and, 65; core curriculum and, 65; crosswalking curriculum and, 64–65; teaching standards blending to, 65

prevention, 7, 56, 71

process evaluation/data, 16, 57–58

professional association, 8–9, 70–72

professional development, supervisor on, 74–76

professional identity, of New Vision School Counselor, 71–72

Professional School Counseling (PSC), on spiritual/religious development, 35

professional school counselor, 70, 78
program evaluation, 55–61, *60*
*Program Evaluation: Methods and
  Case Studies* (Posavac/Carey, R.
  G.), 61
programming, of New Vision School
  Counselor, 68–70
progressive credentials, 74
proximal evaluation, 58
PSC. *See Professional School
  Counseling*
PTSRC. *See* Parent-Teacher-Student
  Resource Center

quasiexperimental research designs,
  59
questions, in needs assessment, 19

referral, 41, 64; for mental health
  services, 4, 30
referral for school counseling
  services: by parent, 91, *92*; by
  teacher/administrator, 91, *91*
reinforcement/reinforcer, 46, 72
release of school counseling case
  notes and sharing of information,
  92–93, *93, 94*
research, 55–61; action, 55, 59;
  collaborative, 57, 65, 67; ethical
  and legal considerations, 61; on
  standards blending, 48. *See also*
  statistical analysis
research-based curriculum
  development, 21–25
research-based practices, 48
research designs, 59
resilience, 32
Response to Intervention (RTI),
  30–31; in comprehensive school
  counseling program, *32*

responsive services, 40; for invisible
  students, 33–34
results reports, 94–96, *95, 96*
risk factors, 32
RTI. *See* Response to Intervention

SCALE. *See* School Counseling
  Analysis, Leadership and
  Evaluation
school: academic mission of, 3,
  13–14, 22; ESEA protection of
  prayer in, 36; reform legislation,
  65
school administrator, 76–77, 91, *91*;
  leadership alliances with, 2,
  12–13; standards-based
  curriculum and, 13
school counseling: ACES and
  CACREP shaping, 6–7; ASCA
  shaping, 10–11; CACREP
  specialty standards, 7; CSCORE
  shaping, 5–6; NBCC shaping,
  7–10; TSCI and ACA shaping,
  3–5. *See also* New Vision School
  Counseling
*School Counseling: A Profession at
  Risk*, ACA report, 1–3
School Counseling Analysis,
  Leadership and Evaluation
  (SCALE) Research Center,
  10–11
School Counseling Operational
  Plan for Effectiveness (SCOPE),
  66, 69, 75; on action and lesson
  planning, 83, *83*
School Counseling Operational
  Report of Effectiveness
  (SCORE), 67, 69, 75, 94–95, *95*;
  on action plans, 83; pre- and post-
  program data worksheet, *96*

school counselor, 27–44; CACREP on clinical competence of, 28; clinical competence, 9, 28, 64; collaboration, 4, 15, 30, 41, 64, 72; as educator, 9–10, 27, 44–46; individual counseling of, 29; individual student planning by, 40; for invisible student, 33–34; NBCC registry of, 8; NCC credential of, 8; noncounseling duties, 77; PBSI, 30–31; on peer programming, 42; as proactive change agents, 4, 42–44, 68; professional, 70, 78; referrals by, 4, 30, 41, 64; responsive services of, 33–34, 40; RTI, 30–31; school administrator leadership alliance with, 2, 12–13; school counseling core curriculum, 40; spiritual/religious development, 34–40; stakeholders and, 43; strengths-based counseling, 31–33. *See also* New Vision School Counselor
School Counselor Competencies, ASCA, 35, 47
school reform initiatives, 11
SCOPE. *See* School Counseling Operational Plan for Effectiveness
SCORE. *See* School Counseling Operational Report of Effectiveness
Search Institute, on developmental assets, 33
self-esteem, research-based curriculum development on, 22–23
small-group curriculum, 51
sole possession case notes, 84
spatial intelligence, 23, *23*

special needs students, needs assessment for, 19–20
specialty counseling, NBCC credentials on, 8
Spiritual and Religious Competencies for School Counselors, 36, *37–39*
spiritual/religious development, 34–40; curriculum, 35; PSC on, 35; student-initiated events participation, 36
stakeholders: action plans and, 83; collaboration and consultation with, 15; needs assessment, 18, 25; school counselor role and, 43; Web site for information to, 43
standards, 47; of CACREP, 73
standards-based curriculum, school administrator and, 13
standards blending, 46–53; achievement gap and, 51–53; alignment approaches, 46–47; beyond the classroom, 69; Bloom's Taxonomy and, 48–49; CACREP and, 65; case illustration, 49–51; for collaboration, 72; curriculum including, 49; multiple intelligences and, 48; research on, 48; systems-focused crosswalking approach, 47, 65; teaching preservice school counselors, 65
statistical analysis, 59
strategies of program evaluation, 56
strengths-based counseling, 31–33
students: academic achievement of, 1–5, 11–14, 46–53, 67–70, 77; holistic development of, 2, 66, 77; values, beliefs, 34–35; worldview, 34–35

students, invisible, 33–34; academic and career planning for, 33; responsive services for, 33–34

substance abuse, 79

suicide ideation, 41, 70, 97; report, 96–98, *97*

summative evaluations. *See* outcome evaluation data

supervisor, 72–76; ASCA on, 78; implementation of school counselor role, 73; NCC, NCSC, LPC credentials of, 78–79; New Vision School Counselor selection by, 73–74; on professional development, 74–76; school counselor roles and functions implementations, 73; selection of, 78–80

systems-focused programming, 3, 29, 63, 68

systems-integration philosophy, 13

teacher: core school counseling curriculum communication to, 86–87; referral for school counseling services, 91, *91*;

school counselor educator and, 46

teaming, 41, 69, 71–72

technology transitioning, 70–71

theory: of learning style, 25; multiple intelligence, *23*, 23–24; practice and, bridging of, 65–67

training program, of NSCTI and NCTSC, 5

Transforming School Counseling Initiative (TSCI), 3–5, 11, 27, 73

triangulation in research, 59

true experimental research designs, 59

TSCI. *See* Transforming School Counseling Initiative

universal academic achievement, 47, 77

violence, peer mediation for reduction of, *60*

Web sites: departmental, 70; for stakeholder information, 43

worldview, of student, 34–35

About the Author

Rita Schellenberg is nationally recognized for her outstanding achievements in education and school counseling. Dr. Schellenberg is professor and director of the school counseling program at Liberty University in Virginia. She received her training in school counseling from the College of William and Mary in Virginia. Dr. Schellenberg was named Outstanding Graduate in her Ph.D. in Counselor Education and Supervision program, and in 2010 she was named one of the top fifteen school counselors in the nation by the American School Counselor Association (ASCA).

Dr. Schellenberg is a licensed school counselor and a licensed professional counselor (LPC). She also holds the credentials of Certified Clinical Mental Health Counselor (CCMHC), Approved Clinical Supervisor (ACS), National Certified Counselor (NCC), National Certified School Counselor (NCSC), and Distance Credentialed Counselor (DCC). Dr. Schellenberg is certified by ASCA as a School Counseling Legal and Ethical Specialist.

Dr. Schellenberg has presented at many conferences on topics related to school counseling and has multiple journal publications in peer-reviewed journals such as *Professional School Counseling.* Dr. Schellenberg is author of *School Counselor's Study Guide for Credentialing Exams* endorsed by the ASCA president.

Dr. Schellenberg engages in consulting for schools and performance consulting for agencies seeking to enhance the performance of children and adolescents. If you would like more information about the author, please visit www.CultivatingPerformance.com.